T0265737

I Have
the Streets

I Have the Streets

A Kutti Cricket Story

R. ASHWIN
and
Sidharth Monga

EBURY
PRESS

An imprint of Penguin Random House

EBURY PRESS

Ebury Press is an imprint of the Penguin Random House group of companies
whose addresses can be found at global.penguinrandomhouse.com

Published by Penguin Random House India Pvt. Ltd
4th Floor, Capital Tower 1, MG Road,
Gurugram 122 002, Haryana, India

First published in Ebury Press by Penguin Random House India 2024

ISBN 9780670094745

Typeset in Sabon LT Std by MAP Systems, Bengaluru, India
Printed at Thomson Press India Ltd, New Delhi

www.penguin.co.in

Foreword

I have played league cricket with Ash in Chennai and Test cricket with him in Australia. He's been my captain in a league team, and I've been his coach in the Indian team. Suffice to say, we've seen each other from close quarters. I've seen the young, talented bowler who made heads turn, the combative teammate just about to hit his prime, and now a seasoned veteran who has constantly reinvented himself during his illustrious career.

I Have the Streets is a vivid and natural extension of the person and cricketer I have known. But it is much more. It is equal parts a cricket book and a children's book. It reminded me of my childhood and not just because I am a professional cricketer and thus find it easier to relate to the stories, the places and the systems a kid goes through to make it as an international cricketer.

This book will have wider appeal because anyone who has ever bowled in a dusty lane will relate to it. So will anyone who has ever dreamed of hitting a match-winning six for their national team; anyone who has juggled studies and sport and spent the last few days before exams in a boot camp of sorts with their friends; and anyone who has looked at their hometown as a living being and not just roads and buildings.

I Have the Streets offers fine insight into why Ash has been so successful. He loves not just the game itself but everything associated with it. He is a cricketing geek—a studious kid who brought his intelligence to the game. He was not naturally the most athletic, but he kept fighting, whether it was the medical challenges he faced as a kid or just to be a better cricketer every single year.

Ash is a perceptive person who appreciates that his parents and granddad have dedicated practically their entire existence to ensuring he becomes the best cricketer he possibly can. But he has managed this well, for he never let this support from his family turn into pressure that shackles him. It is not lost on him how fortunate he is to have grown up in a family that did so much for his cricket without becoming overbearing.

Young kids will envy Ash's unique rise to greatness. These days, they must go through the rigmarole of cricket academies, coaching camps and organized cricket, but he played on the streets and in the neighbourhood parks and nurtured his cricket there. It feels like a forgotten time; not many future superstars of the game will get to learn their cricket this way.

As someone who has shared a dressing room with Ash, I have seen his deep love for his craft. I admire his ability to reflect on it, his willingness to keep working on it, his courage to take risks and his confidence to keep innovating. His love for the game is not merely about finding success, it is about elevating an art form.

At the heart of it all lies a restless competitor. Readers of this book will experience some of the feistiness we have seen on the field and off it. The contest always calls him, and backing down is not in his vocabulary. The true competitor in sport is the one who responds when the conditions are not in his favour. I clearly remember the time when we got a really flat pitch against Australia in Ahmedabad in March 2023. Ash revelled in that challenge and just kept bowling and bowling. Even though the match ended in a draw, he bowled forty-eight overs for six wickets, dipping into his skills, experience and stubbornness.

A year earlier in 2022, when he walked back after helping us win a tight Test with the bat in Bangladesh, I told him, 'Never in doubt, Ash, never in doubt.' I might have said it in a light-hearted way, but it was also the truth: with Ash, you are never in doubt what you are going to get.

As with most successful elite cricketers, this competitiveness can overflow into other situations. He has strong opinions on things and is willing to debate with you. He won't back down from an argument or an issue, but you can see that he's just pushing you and needling you in order to find a way for himself to grow and learn.

I have seen Paras Mhambrey, our bowling coach, occasionally try to impress something upon him. Ash will verbally duel with him, and it never appears that Paras has been able to fully convince him. And yet, two days later, we will see Ash trying the same thing in the nets all by himself. Then we just look at each other, smile and nod: look, he is actually trying to find out why you asked him to do a certain thing. His competitive nature will not let him give you the satisfaction that you convinced him entirely, but in his actions, Ash will show you he has taken it on board.

Ash is quite comfortable in his own company, which is a great trait to have in a cut-throat, high-performance environment. Yet I have seen him grow into a man who enjoys interacting with junior players and passing on what he has learned. With him, knowledge is everything. As a reader, you will see all of this in the book.

I congratulate Ash and wish him all the best for it.

Rahul Dravid

Prologue

It is the summer of 2010 in Madras. The sun seems to be at its peak even at 4 p.m. It doesn't look like it is going to relent any time soon. So, there is no point waiting for it to get cooler. We, young men in our early twenties, are out on 1st Street in Ramakrishnapuram in West Mambalam to play cricket with a tennis ball at this searing hour.

The lamp post is our wicket at the striker's end. At the non-striker's end we have just a stone, which brings another dimension to the cricket: 'current'. If you collect a throw with your foot on the stone, it qualifies as 'breaking the wicket' for run-out purposes, to make up for the smaller target for the fielders. So, we don't need direct hits or accurate throws at the non-striker's end: we just stand with a foot on the stone and collect throws.

Unlike in professional cricket, we allow the last man to bat with a non-striker runner. There is another variation of this rule that gives the last batter a huge advantage. When they bat without a non-striker, they can be run-out only at the end they are running towards. In our street, runs can be scored only on the off side. If you hit over the walls and into a house on the full, you are out.

Another team from another street has made its way to play against us. My friend Bhuvnesh is the captain of our team of five. We have bet a little money to make it more interesting and competitive. The captain of the opposition is a guy named Ashwin.

We usually play five-over games, but this time we are playing it seven-overs-a-side because we have stakes on the match.

I open the batting. I drive into the off side, and run like my life depends on it. Scooters and bikes pass by. A couple of walkers also brave the afternoon sun and venture out on foot. Whenever they come, the game has to come to a brief halt.

There is a hospital at the end of our street. Two overs into the match, a young man walks across with an elderly woman, presumably his mother. We usually try to see if we can help people going to the hospital. This time we assume the son is with her, so we just let them walk by.

This man asks the lady to sit by the temple near the hospital and comes back towards our game of cricket. It is not uncommon to have people stop and see if they can play with us. We assume he is coming to see if he can play, but he waits at a distance and continues to watch us play.

A couple of balls later, he comes even closer. I push and run, and almost run into him as I overrun the stone at the non-striker's end . . . at which point he shouts: 'If only you had done this drop-and-run at Chepauk, Chennai Super Kings would have taken the two points and not be struggling [now].'

He is right. Nine days ago, at Chepauk, I represented Chennai Super Kings, our IPL team, against Kings XI Punjab. I needed to get one run off the last two balls but failed. The match ended in a tie, and we lost the tiebreaker. I have played only one match since. I am not even a part of the larger squad now.

Whenever I lose something in life, when I see no other light, I turn to this cricket in our street with some of my best friends. Everything changes but not the joy I experience when I play here. This inner sanctum now stands infiltrated. This is some journey I have undertaken.

My name is R. Ashwin. Welcome to my world.

1

I can't walk. I can't get up.

That's my oldest memory. I am around five years old. We are at the wedding ceremony of my uncle in Trichy about 330 km from our hometown Madras. I have sat down, but I can't get up. My mother, Amma, is screaming, worried that her son can't get up. My father, Appa, is trying to help me up, but he can't. My parents are panicking. To me, though, my health is not the biggest concern. My fear is, I have brought Amma's brother's wedding to a standstill. I also see other kids running around and playing, which is what children do at weddings. I am feeling left out.

Somehow, they carry me to a doctor. Thankfully the wedding goes ahead. When we return to Madras, we go to the Child Trust Hospital for further assessment. It is discovered that I have a primary complex in my lungs. In simpler terms, I have child tuberculosis (TB). Dr G. Viswanath at Child Trust diagnoses it on the first visit. Each time I am taken to him for treatment, he treats me to a Nutrine candy. The TB is taken care of, but I am left with frequent wheezing attacks.

I don't eat much, but I play a lot. If I eat or drink too much, I vomit. If I run hard, I cough, which leads to vomiting. I play,

I cough, I vomit and I continue playing. On an average, I have wheezing bouts twice a month. Each one lasts six or seven days.

* * *

We don't usually go on family holidays because I attend cricket camps during my summer vacations. This is a rare family holiday that we are going on. We are headed to Kodaikanal, a hill town 525 km south-west of Madras. Trains travelling within Tamil Nadu halt for two minutes at Mambalam Station, near our home in West Mambalam. Appa, though, won't risk boarding the train in two minutes, so we make the long journey to the originating station—Madras Egmore. We have packed all our food for the journey. We are all excited.

The moment we board the train, though, I start vomiting. By the time the train reaches Mambalam Station, my parents have decided I am too sick to travel. We use that two-minute halt to alight and head back home. And then the hospital. We miraculously manage to get all our luggage off in those two minutes. The journey to the station has lasted longer than the holiday. This time, I have malaria.

My health is a source of constant worry for my parents, especially my father. Appa is tall, he has a lush moustache and he rides a Bullet. My parents' friend Antony lives with us while he studies to be a chartered accountant. The CA institute is near our home. Antony is around the same age as my parents, but he is more of a friend to me. I confide in him more than I do in my parents. When he gets a job in Dubai, we all go to Bombay to see him off. When he returns, he brings a pair of aviators for Appa and binoculars for me.

I wear them around my neck and sit on my father's bike. Appa is wearing his new aviators. We have variety rice, snacks and cola packed with us, and we are riding to Chepauk to watch my first Test match live. India are playing England in early 1993 at MA Chidambaram Stadium in Madras, which is more commonly known as Chepauk, the locality it sits in.

Appa works in the accounts section of the Indian Railways. His father, Thatha to me, a former Railways employee himself, asked him to apply for the job. Appa always dresses in a formal shirt, formal trousers, a belt and polished shoes. Always proper. When he rides his Bullet, sporting his new aviators, policemen salute Appa.

Appa loves his cricket. He is a lower-division league cricketer, a fast bowler. I am told he is a very good tennis-ball cricketer as well. My oldest memory of cricket is watching him take a wicket on a weekend. He bowled out somebody, sending the bail flying. He didn't celebrate much, but I remember his teammates walking towards him to congratulate him. Old-school pros. For the games, he leaves home in his whites. He doesn't have a kitbag. He carries his bat between both his pads, which are strapped around each other; the gloves are strapped at the top. I want to copy his bowling action, although I am more of a batter.

We are lucky to have Pavilion Terrace tickets to enjoy a straight view of the action at Chepauk. Sachin Tendulkar bats with a Slazenger bat, which the hapless England attack struggles to go past. A shot that stays with me is an Alec Stewart clip off Kapil Dev. We are sitting next to a travelling English supporter. Appa spends a lot of time talking to him about the defence of Geoffrey Boycott. The defence of the current side is not good enough to deny Anil Kumble and India an innings win. Appa also takes me to the commentary box to get me an autograph from Sunil Gavaskar.

The everlasting memory I come back from Chepauk with is the stench of pan masala and chewing-tobacco. That's the first thing about Chepauk. First the stench, then the stains, then the cricket. What cricket. It is magical to watch it from the ground.

I want to play cricket, too. Appa, too, wants me to play. He is mad about the sport, and now he has an accomplice. A year ago, he spent a fortune—his salary had just jumped from Rs 700 to Rs 1900 thanks to the pay commission—to buy an Onida colour TV in time for us to watch the World Cup from Australia. Much to the annoyance of Amma, who was not even consulted. Early in the morning, he would invite the neighbours, make them tea and then watch the matches with them. I would wake up too, but I wasn't as big a fan of watching it on TV as I was when we went to Chepauk.

Appa enrols me at the YMCA because I am getting too front-on in my back-foot defence. A friend of his, a Railways Ranji player, is the coach at the YMCA. Where I go for it may be Appa's choice, but that I am going for cricket coaching is at my mother's insistence. Amma works at HLL. She is from the historical town of Sirkazhi, but she studied in Trichy and moved to Madras after marriage. She doesn't want me out on the streets on Sundays, the only day she is at home. She wants some structure in my cricket, and she wants to be able to see me on Sundays.

Amma is better at making these decisions. She looks much younger than Appa. She is tall and pretty, in complete contrast to Appa's rugged look. And yet, if I wake her up during her Sunday afternoon nap—the only one she gets all week—she can let go of all the delicateness. This is a reminder of how hard she works during the week and how much she values her 'me' time. She is strong and resourceful. She is always looking for ways to acquire new skills so she can help provide for the family better.

The dedication to follow through with such decisions, though, comes from Appa. Thatha didn't allow him to pursue cricket because he didn't earn enough to raise the family and also provide for his cricketing needs. Appa doesn't want the same to happen to me. His biggest worry is our orthodox extended family. Sometimes, even Thatha tells him cricket is not going to put food on my plate. Other relatives are worse.

'Why are you sending him out to play in the sun?'

'He has got another wheezing attack.'

'What about his studies? All his cousins are doing so well.'

* * *

I am scared of Appa at the best of times, but as my exams approach, my fear reaches a fever pitch. I study at Padma Seshadri

Bala Bhavan, a school known more for its academic exploits than for the athletes who study there. It is no accident. The impetus for exam scores is unmissable. When the results are in, your name is called out loud in front of the rest of the class, followed by your scores. Casual snide remarks are thrown in if you haven't done well.

'If you had come to school more often, you would have scored better marks.'

'Go tell your father how "well" you have done.'

Appa doesn't need that pressure reinforced. He knows his own family will be after him if I don't do well. So, he studies what I have to study and then teaches it to me. He reads all my textbooks. He finds out what notes I am missing. He then goes to my classmates' houses to borrow notes. He sits there, writes them in his notebook and then brings them home.

Appa is not easily pleased. He wants to get them from the best of the students. He wants to find out their secret while he is writing down the notes. Not every parent is nice.

'Why your son didn't write?'

'What is the problem?'

'Is your son okay?'

'Why don't you take him to a doctor?'

That doesn't deter Appa. He prepares question papers to give me a mock exam before the actual exam. He puts a clock in front of me and sits right next to me for three hours. If he has to go somewhere, he makes someone—Thatha or the domestic help— watch me. Sometimes he bluffs and leaves me alone to check from the window if I am cheating.

Appa hates cheating. Everything has to be done the right way. Every person has to be straightforward. Every morning he tells me three things: 'You should not lie. You should not steal from others. You should not harm others.'

But I end up lying. He somehow gets hold of the question paper by the time I return and asks me the answers I wrote. This is what I fear about him. He has hardly ever hit me, but he talks and talks and talks. He reasons and reasons and reasons. It is impossible to get the better of him when he gets into arguments. It is getting close to 4 p.m., which is the time we start playing cricket in the street. At a time when cricket is the only thing that matters in the world. So, I lie to him, saying I have done well in the exam. I tell him I have answered the questions exactly as he told me to. I know he is eventually bound to find out, but that confrontation can wait. Right now, I can't see past the cricket.

* * *

I don't want to miss playing cricket in the front yard for anything. The sunlight is precious; it dips quickly on the east coast. There are accidents aplenty. One of us hits a ball into a neighbour's well. It's never good news if the ball goes into a well. One of two things can happen: either there is water in the well or there isn't. It is hard to say which is better.

If there is water, there is hope of retrieving the ball, but we have to go through the arduous process of begging the owners of the house for a rope and a bucket. First, you convince Aunty to get you a bucket. Every older lady is 'Aunty' in India, and every man 'Uncle'. You don't need to be related. While Aunty looks for the bucket, she keeps badmouthing us.

'We drink this water and you have thrown a dirty ball into it.'

'Can't you go play in a park?'

'Why don't you study?'

After what seems like twenty minutes, she emerges with a bucket, but the rope is with Uncle. Then you find the Uncle and convince him to lend you the rope.

'*Kayiru batharam ah thirripi varanum.*'

The rope should come back in the same state as it was when given to you. By now, you are on the verge of tears.

You still need a Thatha from the house to follow you because you can't be left near the well without adult supervision. Before you know it, the sun has set.

When the well is dry, as it is today, you have to wait for the rain before you can even try to retrieve the ball. You run home and ask your parents for the money to buy a new ball, but your parents are not home at this time of the day. So, you go to Thatha and ask him for money to buy a new ball. Good luck with that. He clearly remembers paying for the last ball, too. He refuses to pay until every other house has bought us a ball each.

Thatha is, after all, his son's father. But he is a harder taskmaster and a stricter disciplinarian. Everything must be streamlined. No deviations. If you want to play, he will play with you. Chess, carrom, whatever, but you must play seriously. No fooling around. He even goes and watches the games of Anthony Maria Irudayam, the carrom champion, and tries to show me his tricks.

Thatha was a wrestler when he was young. Once he foiled a theft attempt at home. Thatha, his brother and his mother were all sleeping in the same room when they saw an iron rod with a hook being dangled from a hole in the asbestos roof. Thatha's brother grabbed the rod, and Thatha chased and caught hold of the thief when he tried to escape. Just when Thatha was handing the thief over to the police, the thief threatened him: 'I have seen your face now, I won't let this slide.'

Sure enough, the thief started stalking Thatha after he came out. Thatha worked on the tracks and not in an office. The thief must have felt Thatha was vulnerable. After this went on for days, Thatha led him into an isolated alley. The moment the thief entered the lane, he locked the thief's hands and broke one of his fingers. The stalking ended there.

Thatha moved into a separate portion of the house to give my parents their space. He cooks his own meals, although Appa remains the best cook I have known. All of Thatha's food intake is measured: a certain amount of garlic in the morning and a certain amount of milk. His meal portions are never larger than one bowl. He tends to his plants from 6 a.m. to 8 a.m. every day. Once every month, he picks up his Atlas bicycle and leaves at 5 a.m. He returns home in the evening after spending the day getting a full-body check-up at the Railway Hospital.

Thatha doesn't want Amma to quit her job. When she says she is worried about my wheezing attacks, Thatha assures her he will look after me. He believes Amma's strength lies in working, and she should not let go of it. I spend a lot of time with him when my parents are away. He has installed a gunny sack on his bike carrier for me to sit on. My school, about three kilometres from home, ends at 3 p.m.; he is there at 2.50 p.m. If I have cricket practice, he brings me milk and biscuits and then drops me off at the practice after I've had the mini meal. He sits around for a while, reading his newspaper, and leaves once he has made sure I am okay at the practice. Appa picks me up from practice. If I don't have cricket practice, Thatha brings me home, gives me lunch and makes sure I sleep for a while before the 4 p.m. gully cricket.

Thatha watches all four tennis Grand Slams with me. During the French Open, he teaches me that *egalité* is a synonym for deuce, but its literal meaning is equality. He knows many languages: Tamil, Malayalam, Telugu, Kannada, Tulu, Hindi, French, English. He makes sure I watch the English news, and he teaches me how to read maps. Thatha doesn't need any maps when he takes me to Bangalore for my first cricket tour.

At the age of nine, I am asked to play for the Under-14 side of a club called TSR, one of the academies I go to. Appa believes in repetition for a batter: you play seven days a week and you bat as long as you can. He has even enrolled me at another school's practice—St John's, Besant Nagar—because it doesn't have a specialist cricket coach and is, thus, less crowded. TSR are missing one player so they ask if I will go to Bangalore for the Anand Sweets tournament.

Karnataka tournaments are well known for their quality, Appa says. Teams come from Hyderabad, Madras, Bombay and Bangalore. My parents somehow arrange for the money required to send me there, but neither can get time off from their respective jobs. So, I go with Thatha. We stay in the Karnataka State Cricket Association dormitory at the Chinnaswamy Stadium. Opposition teams feature school-cricket prodigies such as Robin Uthappa, Gaurav Dhiman and Pawan Gargi.

I am mostly giving throwdowns to senior boys. I get picked in the XI, but mostly for my fielding. I barely get the opportunity to bat in the tournament. T.S. Ramaswamy, owner of the club, comes all the way from Madras to watch us play in the semi-final.

He is a well-known lawyer and cricket patron, and a magnanimous person. He rewards every player who scores a hundred or takes five wickets with Rs 500. Again, I don't get the opportunity to bat, but on the field, I stop a few forceful shots at short midwicket, saving our team precious runs. I even run a batter out with a direct hit.

After the match, Ramaswamy makes it a point to praise my fielding and rewards me with Rs 500 in front of everyone. It's so different from having your exam scores read out in front of everybody. This game is not bad.

2

'Aunty, your son ran away as soon as he got out.'

'Uncle, send your son out to finish the game that he ran away from.'

At eight, I am notorious in our lane for running into houses and dragging kids out to complete our games of cricket. More than a sweetly timed shot or the sight of flying stumps, it is the competition that has attracted me to cricket. I cannot bear to play a game of cricket that is not competitive. Make it interesting, and I can play Test matches in our narrow street. If, on the other hand, a neighbour doesn't play seriously, he is not welcome to our games of cricket. Even if his parents come and try to convince us, we refuse to involve him. I introduce a nominal one- or two-rupee participation fee to make sure everyone is serious about the games.

We live in a narrow lane in Ramakrishnapuram, in the West Mambalam locality of southern Madras. It is an old neighbourhood with old houses, which means plenty of open spaces to play cricket in. There are trees to dodge and wells to avoid, but it only adds to the fun. We avoid playing in the street and use the big house next door instead. Their front yard has a mud floor and is big enough for a 16-yard pitch, a small run-up for the bowler and a wicketkeeper between the stumps and the compound wall. The bigger boys bowl fast, and all the boys are big.

My actual Aunty—Appa's sister—and her family live with us.

Her elder son is Sriram, a gifted athlete. He mainly plays football, kicks the ball a long way and also takes part in 100-metre and 200-metre sprints. On one occasion our school's team is one short, we take along Sriram, who has never played with a cricket ball. The match is against St John's Besant Nagar at Don Bosco in Egmore. Since the player missing is an opener, we send Sriram to open. He flicks the first ball of the match for a six. He scores a quick fifty, and bowls at a good pace.

The school coach approaches Appa to see if Sriram, too, can be sent for cricket coaching. Appa tries to convince Sriram's parents, but the conversation ends up being an unpleasant one. Sriram's parents want him to focus more on his studies and less on sports. They don't want Appa to introduce him to 'wasteful' activities. He is allowed to play our gully cricket, though.

Sriram, and his younger brother Shyam, join us every day. Three boys from the house next to ours and three from the one opposite ours are always present. I am the youngest, and for a long time, they have resisted including me in their games out of fear that I could get hurt. However, I have proved my utility to them by bowling fast. Gradually, they let me bat.

You can't survive Ramakrishnapuram 1st Street gully cricket if you can't play the pull shot. For starters, you will have to run all your runs if you can't hit to square leg. The way we play, there are glass windows behind the bowler. So, to disincentivize hitting towards the windows, we award no boundaries for straight hits. This is where—to score boundaries and not run my runs—I develop an affinity for the pull shot.

You have to be careful with the pull shot, though: if you fail to keep it down, the ball sails over the boundary wall and goes into the temple next door. That is one of the popular modes of dismissal. Another is to get an edge on a delivery fast enough to rise and clear the boundary wall behind the batter. Then there is the lbw. Because we always fight over the umpire's decision on lbw, we have simplified the rule: if you get hit on the leg three times, you are out lbw.

We need all these modes of dismissal because we are playing unlimited overs, and the severely competitive boys can bat on cussedly, often taking games into the next day. Especially the lbw. The big boys are fast, and they aim for the legs. I know if Manu, for example, hits my toe, I will come down like a sack of potatoes. So, I start at a young age to keep my legs out of the way and play balls into the off side. Playing these 'Test' matches, two foundations of my batting have already been laid: if it is short, I pull; if it is full, I stay beside the line to prevent getting hit on the leg.

I fine-tune it in the underarm version of our cricket, which we play the day after our unlimited-overs matches. This is a softer version born out of necessity—played in a smaller portico of sorts—but also more skilled. Boys do wonderful things with the ball between their fingers. It swings and turns in an unpredictable manner. To score on the off side, you must split two pillars, for which you have to play with an open face. This is how I start playing most of the spin bowling. Underarm games are played over limited overs and are not carried forward to the next day.

We don't need planning, communication or acknowledgement. Through some magical coordination, we are all always there by 4 p.m. Every time I fail, I am mocked for not being good enough to succeed in neighbourhood matches despite going to cricket coaching. When I do well, I make sure to walk with a swagger. Competitiveness often gets the better of me, resulting in broken windows. Every time a window breaks and kids disappear into their own houses, Uncles and Aunties first contact Appa because I am the likeliest culprit.

After our matches, we talk about our matches. Sometimes we talk about the match played the previous week. Especially particular shots. If Sachin Tendulkar has stepped out and hit Glenn McGrath back over his head, we are all imitating him, even if we get out doing so. We discuss Sachin's interview, where he is asked what he did differently when playing that audacious shot. He says he just looked to play straight. So, for that week or so, we all keep playing straight. And nodding a little, just like Sachin, if we connect.

This gully cricket is the foundation of our friendships. Outside of these games, we don't know much about each other. Even if we go to the same schools, we are not in the same classes.

* * *

Amma's office suddenly assumes special importance in March 1998. Any one of HLL's products is usually a sponsor of Test cricket in India, which means complimentary tickets for its employees when cricket comes to Madras. And this is not just any cricket. This is the biggest battle of our times: Sachin Tendulkar against Shane Warne. Australia are visiting India for a Test series after twelve years.

We have been reading in the newspapers that Sachin has asked L. Sivaramakrishnan, who last played for India in 1987 but is still turning out for Tamil Nadu, to help him prepare for Warne. For forty-five minutes, twice daily, Siva just bowls into the rough outside leg to simulate Warne for Sachin. If this is so huge for Sachin, it is even bigger for us.

Weeks in advance, Appa and I have asked Amma to request tickets from her office. Her office, too, has a huge demand for tickets. They draw up a priority list, which Amma misses because the managers usually get the best tickets. So, she finds out who is getting those tickets and approaches those managers to request them. Meanwhile, Appa starts to queue up outside ticket centres the day the ticket window opens. Just in case we don't get the complimentary ones, you know, he buys two cheaper tickets as a backup.

With each passing day in the week before the Test match, the anticipation builds up. During school, I make plans for how we will watch and what we will take to the ground. I want to carry packed snacks and a big bottle of Pepsi with me because Sachin appears in the cold drink's advertisements. I have dusted off the binoculars Antony brought from Dubai.

A couple of days before the match, I start pestering Appa for money to buy Pepsi and chips because I don't want it to get too hectic on the morning of the match. Appa, though, keeps putting it off. The money for these treats has not been accounted for in the monthly budget, which means he has to ask Thatha. And Thatha is already giving him a hard time for deciding to make me skip school for a week. He dreads another debate, so he wants to do it on the morning of the match when there is less time for one.

By now, the Bullet has given way to a more economical family man's ride: a Hero Honda CD 100. Like the donkey from *Shrek*, I keep asking him every two minutes, 'How far is Chepauk now?' When we hit the Gemini flyover, Appa points me to Tarapore Towers and its MRF-sponsored temperature display.

MRF (Madras Rubber Factory) runs a world-famous fast-bowling academy in Madras and also sponsors a select few cricketers' bats. Sachin is their current choice. Tarapore Towers is a corporate office building. One of the offices inside the Towers is India Cements, which basically runs cricket in Madras. And then Appa tells me, 'When you can see Tarapore Towers, it means Chepauk is not far.' Indeed, it isn't.

Down Mount Road, make a right at Anna Statue, head towards Marina Beach and on the way is the stadium. We hit a red light on Mount Road, near the tomb of Syed Moosa Sha Khaderi. Not for the first time, I see a traffic policeman salute Appa. And he responds too. I find it funny but don't ask him what is going on.

It is like we have come to a festival or a fair. The conches are going off, people are giving away those free golf caps made of paper and vehicles are being stopped well before the ground. So, we enter one of the bylanes in Triplicane, a congested neighbourhood full of eateries, lodges and small businesses, and ask one of the homeowners if we can park the bike there. 'At your own risk,' we are told.

At this time, we don't mind taking the risk. We need to start walking towards Chepauk as soon as possible. First, we get hold of the fours and sixes wagons. They allow us to take our food inside. So, there we are, armed with all our Pepsi, crisps, tomato rice or curd rice packed by Amma, all ready to be enchanted by the magic that awaits us. Of course, there is always an orientation period during which you get acclimatized to the chewing-tobacco stench, the quintessential Chepauk smell.

Mark Taylor sets an aggressive field for Sachin. Immediately, it is Tendulkar vs Warne. First ball, four. Fifth ball, caught at slip. The crowd at Chepauk gives a hard time to boundary fielders Gavin Robertson and Michal Slater. They keep calling out the players' names to get their attention, and then they boo at them and call them names when they turn around. We believe this has an adverse effect on their performance.

Sachin shows the value of the practice he has put in when he attacks Warne in the second innings from out of the rough and against the turn to totally deflate Australia.

Ten months later, Madras gets an even bigger game. It's the first Test between India and Pakistan in ten years. Wasim Akram, Saeed Anwar and Inzamam-ul-Haq are going to play in front of our eyes at our own Chepauk. A full house watching India play Pakistan for the first time in a decade. Anil Kumble taking wickets, Saqlain Mushtaq's *doosras*, a whirlwind century by Shahid Afridi only for Venkatesh Prasad to keep India alive.

Nadeem Khan, Pakistan's left-arm spinner, is like Kumar Dharmasena in the mirror. A mix of Dharmasena and Phil Tufnell, actually. I have seen a lot of Tufnell in the matches from Australia. England tend to lose every time, and poor Tufnell tends to just bowl and bowl. Yousuf Youhana's SS pads remind me of mine: bulging from the sides, as if too big for his legs. Sachin gets him out in both innings.

Tamil Nadu's own Sadagoppan Ramesh, making his debut, lays into Wasim Akram and Waqar Younis on the first evening. We have not seen any batter in this Test walk in and feel at ease because of the bounce in the pitch. Ramesh looks like he is batting on a different surface. His innings doesn't continue for long on the second morning, but these are 43 stylish runs that we have thoroughly enjoyed in the stands. Besides, when he gets out, it brings Sachin to the middle.

When Saqlain gets Sachin duck-out in the first innings, I tell everyone in our stand that he will score a century in the second.

Because he did so against Australia after he failed to beat their superstar spinner in the first innings.

My head is buzzing as we head to Chepauk for Day Four, with India needing 231 with eight wickets in hand. We have great seats right behind the bowler's arm, but the damn queue is not moving. We enter a little late, and the moment my head pops up to watch, the ball has already left Wasim Akram's hand. It is an unplayable ball. Rahul Dravid is bowled. The chewing-tobacco smell, Akram's whippy release, movement in the air, and then off the pitch, the flying off bail. The moment is frozen in my mind.

By the time we settle, Sourav Ganguly has been given out caught, even though the ball has touched the ground at least twice. Madras' own V.K. Ramaswamy is the square-leg umpire who helps New Zealander Steve Dunne make the decision. Our entire stand starts chanting, 'Ramaswamy down.'

With India heading for a defeat, there is so much tension in the stands that no one ventures close to the boundary to heckle the Pakistan players. This usually happens at Chepauk. When India are doing well, we lay into the opposition fielders. Not so much when India are struggling. Sachin and Nayan Mongia drag India out, giving us a voice, hope and eventually belief.

Then Mongia skies a pull. Sachin finally makes a mistake, and the rest can't get us the remaining 17 runs. We are shocked into silence once again. Then, when Pakistan's players are walking back after shaking hands with the Indian team players, the Pavilion Terrace starts applauding them. Taken aback at first, Wasim Akram responds by applauding that section of the crowd. We all start moving closer and respond with another cheer. Before we know it, Pakistan decide to go on a victory lap, to applause from the whole stadium.

* * *

Amma is not the only one with useful connections when it comes to us watching live cricket matches. Appa's Railways job means getting train tickets is not a hassle. So we keep travelling to Bangalore and Bombay to watch Test matches. A trip to Bombay is an elaborate affair. We leave on the Dadar Express two days before the Test. Every meal for the train journey is cooked, packed and carried from home. We don't buy any food on the way. We have relatives in Ghatkopar, and Appa has a friend near Dharavi.

Appa is particular about us not burdening them. So, we stagger our stay and don't bother them for food, etc. Our day starts early in the morning. A mess in Dadar is our first stop. An idli costs a rupee and fifty paise here. We get our breakfast here and also switch from the central to the western line of the Mumbai local trains. Appa knows all about the confusing system. Churchgate, the neighbourhood that houses Wankhede Stadium, is also on the western line and the last stop. We can see snaking queues from the train even before it stops at Churchgate.

We can't afford seats with a straight view here, but we don't mind the side view. Appa makes sure to also take me to the Police Gymkhana to watch club matches when we have the time. In the evening, we get off at Dadar station and walk to Shivaji Park, Sachin's first playground and host to many simultaneous games of cricket in the evening.

Cricket is the bond between Appa and me. If we're not watching matches together at Chepauk or stadiums in Bangalore and Bombay, we're watching them on cable TV. While other kids my age struggle to watch the sport, I get a free pass thanks to Appa. The second half of the games being telecast from Sharjah, England and South Africa is a good opportunity for Appa to watch with me. Games from the West Indies are perfect as they start after 7 p.m. He is back home from work, and I am back from playing cricket.

Being tired, I am prone to falling asleep midway. Often, I am woken up from deep sleep by Appa lest I miss a good game. When Sachin single-handedly carries India to the final of the Sharjah Cup in 1998, I'm already asleep because of the desert-storm break. I wake up to wild cheering from Appa, Amma, Antony and my cousins.

Another time, in 1999, Appa wakes me up well past midnight. I have given up on this game from Barbados, but Brian Lara is up to something special in the final-innings chase against Australia. It is surreal to watch. It is almost magical. He doesn't make a single mistake; he looks incapable of making one. He shepherds two hopeless tailenders to take West Indies to an unbelievable one-wicket win. The next morning, I wake up with a stomach ache. Appa knows I just want to miss school so I can watch the highlights, and he allows me to. Appa hates lies, but for some reason, this lie is okay.

The next year, I miss India's win in the Port-of-Spain Test because it is too late at night. Another stomach ache the following morning. Appa knows. There is no need to wink.

* * *

I am ten when Appa's teammates at Egmore Excelsiors ask him to bring me around to play for them. I have been taking formal coaching, and my batting is coming along nicely. Appa fears I will get hit by the hard cricket ball, so he keeps resisting. I am not puny, but I don't have the muscle mass to go with my height. With all my wheezing and vomiting bouts, I struggle to keep any food down. Two years later, he finally gives in.

At twelve, I make my Madras leagues debut for Egmore Excelsiors in the fifth division. My first kitbag is the same improvised pads-around-the-bat contraption. The bat is Appa's Simon Tuskers, fully taped and gutted. In my second season, I have scored a century. My main utility, though, is to field at slip and short leg. I take a lot of catches. And blows, because fifth-division spinners are quite erratic with their discipline, thus endangering their short-leg fielders.

Now, instead of protecting me from the cricket ball, Appa is following the coaches' advice that tennis-ball cricket will ruin my game. So, he tries to ration those matches for me. To help me rid myself of the fear, he installs a net in the house. The surface of the first one is quite rough, so he gets it redone to a smooth finish. During a family function at home, he asks the videographer to film me while batting. It comes back like a wedding film.

Appa throws balls at me from a close distance so that I don't fear the thirty- to forty-year-old pros in the leagues, who can be a terror with the unpredictable bounce of the matting pitches we get in the fifth division.

Batting against them is not even the scariest part. It is the fear of letting your teammates down and getting admonished for it. The first season is really intimidating. I'm not sure what they will say or where they will make me stand on the field. I keep fearing misfielding or dropping a catch. No matter how poorly the team has bowled, if a young kid makes a mistake on the field, that kid becomes the reason they lost. They make you run from deep midwicket to deep cover between balls. To score a hundred and compete against these men in just one year tells me I might have something in me as a cricketer.

Appa recognizes it and wants me to be tested against the best. He gets me enrolled in as many academies as he can. Some coaches he pays; others he takes favours from, using his connections. Former India wicketkeeper Bharath Reddy now handles operations at Chemplast. As the name suggests, it is a chemical company in Madras. The name doesn't give away, though, that they field two strong teams in the higher divisions of the Madras leagues: Jolly Rovers and Alwarpet CC. He also runs his own academy, where I train.

By thirteen, I am a bit of a big dog at the Bharath Reddy Academy. Appa is tempted to get me to the seniors' nets, among the Jolly Rovers probables, to test me. One of the quicks knocking at the Jolly Rovers door is L. Balaji, who is unplayable on matting pitches. He bowls rockets that don't even come straight at you. His outswingers are hard to follow; his inswingers hit batters in the chest and not the pads.

The thing with Appa, though, is that he will never undermine a coach by making such a demand. A coach is almost like a senior police officer whose orders must be followed without question. The other thing about Appa is that he will not give up. When this inner conflict of his becomes apparent, Amma comes to the rescue by offering to make that call to Bharath Reddy. However, Bharath Reddy still ends up giving Appa a piece of his mind when he sees us. Facing Balaji at thirteen is a death wish, he says.

Appa is slightly bolder at the other academy, Sishya, run by P.K. Dharmalingam, who does cricket shows on TV. He is the man Kapil Dev credits with teaching him how to take catches running back and over his shoulder, the most famous one being that of Viv Richards in the 1983 World Cup final. After two months of persistence, Appa finally convinces Dharmalingam to let me bat against the senior quicks. There is no sight screen; we are on a matting surface with concrete underneath, and this big, fast bowler runs in. The first ball I face hits me in the chest, and I am down. I have to be carried out of the nets.

For a few days after the incident, I wake up in the middle of the night to see a hand near my nose and mouth. It's Appa checking to see if I am still breathing. He feels guilty and is worried about pushing me too far. He scales it back a little but doesn't give up on repetitions. Repetition to build muscle memory is a big thing with him. A day before I have a match, he sits on a sofa and keeps throwing balls at me. At least 200. 'Bend that knee when you play the cover-drive.' He has also tied a ball to a rope that hangs from the ceiling so that I can keep repeating my shots. This way, I don't need a person to throw balls at me, nor do I need someone to run after the ball.

There is one problem, though: the ball keeps hitting the fridge before coming back to me. This fridge was gifted to Thatha by his father-in-law when it was rare for homes to have one. Thatha continues to treasure it. The fridge has become the trigger for the outpouring of all the tension between Thatha and Appa. Thatha doesn't like Appa investing so much time, money and emotion in my cricket. Especially with my health problems.

On this one day, I am getting in a last-minute knock before a league game. As I keep hitting the fridge, tempers flare between Thatha and Appa, who cushions me from it.

'You have no value for money. You don't know how expensive this fridge is.'

In an attempt to shield the fridge, Appa tries to get in the way of a shot I play, but my bat swing ends at his forehead, splitting it open. Immediately, blood gushes out. The floor turns red. I freeze, drop the bat and stand there not knowing what to do.

Appa doesn't react. He just walks to the hospital at the end of our lane, gets some first aid, comes back, picks up my kitbag, places it on his bike's fuel tank and takes me to the match.

During our ride to the ground, Appa doesn't say a word. I sit there, wondering what mistakes I have made. I could have stopped hitting the fridge when they were fighting. I could have pulled out of my swing when I saw Appa moving towards the fridge. Why is Appa not speaking to me? Is he that angry? And if he is that angry, why is he taking me to the match?

By the time I finish the game and see him, Appa has already found out that I have scored a fifty. Still no words from him. He places the bag back on the fuel tank and takes me to a bakery, where he treats me to some cake.

After all that, Appa finally speaks: 'I shed blood this morning for your cricket, but you scored only a fifty. You should make it count and score hundreds.'

* * *

I realize Appa has over-dramatized a straightforward cricketing message: score big when you get in. He is not the sort to pile on the pressure of expectation. For all the broken windows he has had to pay for, for all the fights he's had with relatives, for all the notes he's got for me, for all the mock tests he has given me, Appa has never let it show. He doesn't need to. It is plain to me how the life of everyone in the family revolves around me and my cricket.

I feel good about how my cricket is progressing. The homoeopathic treatment has either worked or my body has recovered by itself, but my wheezing attacks have finally stopped. At fourteen, I am representing Madras against a combined Tamil Nadu districts team in Tirunelveli. In one of the games, I stretch to defend a ball off the front foot, and I feel something has twisted. Immediately, I feel pain. For the rest of the game, I am unable to run. I limp even when walking. Still, I field in the slips and take seven catches.

I don't make much of it and return to normal cricket activity in Madras. My back, though, has begun to act up. Every once in a while it gets stiff, but I don't tell anyone. I am getting ready for my next cricket tour. I have been selected to play for Tamil Nadu in the South Zone Under-14 tournament. If you perform well here, you get selected for the South Zone team, so there is a fair bit of competition among us teammates.

We first travel to Goa, a game you don't want to miss. Goa and Kerala are the weaker sides against whom you can score tons of runs. Even though every selector knows this, somehow aggregate runs matter when teams are picked. In Goa, I am asked to run a lap around the ground. I am not sure if it is the stiff back or if someone else needs to play this easy game, but I am declared unfit after running that one lap. My friend R.A. Aravind opens in my absence, along with our captain Anirudha Srikkanth, son of former India captain Kris Srikkanth.

Anirudha comes across as a privileged kid. He arrives for training in a car. He speaks good English. His demeanour is snobbish. He is a bit of a bully, who makes fun of several other people. However, I refuse to take a step backwards, which sparks fights between us. The beauty of Anirudha, though, is that he can put all this behind him on the cricket field and be a really good teammate and captain. The next match is against Karnataka, our strongest rivals in the South Zone, at CPTI Pistons Ground in Madras. I am declared fit for this game. Aravind is dropped for this match altogether, Anirudha moves to No. 3, and the No. 3 from the last game, B. Sriram, walks out to open with me. This brings me face to face once again with Gaurav Dhiman, who has developed into a pretty good all-rounder. In three days, Dhiman gets me duck-out twice. In the first innings, I last six balls; in the second, three.

In the evening, they inform me that I don't need to return for the next game. I find it insensitive that they can't even wait for kids to get home and process the match before they are told they are dropped. Appa picks me up on his bike, and all through the ride home, he has tens of questions about the game. I want some quiet because I am just contemplating my future, not just in the game but in the world. In between giving cursory replies to Appa's questions, these thoughts are running through my mind:

'Okay, what have we got over here? I'm not a great student. I am not going to become an astronaut. I don't think I can be a doctor. What does it take to be an engineer? Math. And I'm not great at it either. So, what am I going to do? I'm already a very ordinary student, whereas all my classmates are great. And I thought cricket was going to be one of my sparks in life, or my everything in life, and I'm not great at it either. At fourteen, I'm not able to dominate. When am I going to dominate? I am probably just a small-time school cricketer who has dominated school cricket, and I've lived in my small pond, and now the reality has hit me. So, what lies in front of me? Am I going to be a failure? My parents aren't very well off. Maybe they expect me to lift this family; maybe they don't.'

The ride home is a blur, and the moment I see Amma, I put my head in her lap and break down. I blurt out what is going through my head, and I apologize for letting the whole family down. She tells me, 'Listen, I'm working extra hours. I don't even see you some days because you are asleep even before I come home. Why do you think I'm doing it? Because I want you to pursue your passion. You go and play the game. I will earn as much as I can. So even if you become a failure in life, it will take care of you. Go and enjoy the game. I never had the opportunity. In fact, if my father had seen his grandson playing cricket when he was alive, he would have sold everything he had to put the money into your game. He'll be very happy wherever he is. You have everyone's blessings, don't worry.'

Amma puts me at ease, but the next morning, I wake up in terrible pain and begin limping again. Now, the family begins to mobilize all its resources. Amma calls up her sister, a gynaecologist who works in Nigeria. She knows a doctor in Madras and sets up an appointment. Next, I find myself in the government hospital right next to the one where I was born. It doesn't take long to find out that my hip disc has slipped. The doctor says they will have to surgically open it, release the pressure on the nerve roots and then screw it up. He also foresees the bone growing in a couple of years and expects another surgery to be required then.

My parents' whole world has come crashing down. This is going to bring its own financial strain, but more ominously, two surgeries before the age of sixteen or seventeen will mean my cricket is done for. For the last four to five years, my parents' and Thatha's lives have all revolved around my cricket. They have worked hard within their limited means to get a perennially sick child to play cricket. Amma is determined to do all she can even if I fail, but now I won't even have a chance to fail. Appa has found time to take me to games and practically pass my exams himself. Despite his reservations, Thatha has been there to look after me and my cricket whenever Appa and Amma are busy. My cricket has kept my family busy. Now it is all over. Now there is nothing to do.

3

Appa is not the type to give up easily. He takes me to another orthopaedic doctor. This one advises two surgeries: one to open my hip and the other to open my back. The consolation here is that there won't be a need to install a screw if we go with these two surgeries. So, we break open Amma's and Thatha's savings and secure a loan to finance the surgery.

On the day of the surgery, when Amma informs her boss that she needs the second half of the day off, her boss asks her why she looks upset. When she tells him about the surgery, he insists we see the chief orthopaedic surgeon of Apollo Hospital. He knows the man, Dr Gopalakrishnan, and squeezes in an appointment on the same afternoon. With the other doctor waiting, we head over to Apollo with the X-ray and MRI scans. Immediately, Dr Gopalakrishnan asks us to call off the surgery because I am too young for one. And he says there is a contusion between the hips, which should go away with rest.

This sudden turn of events brings relief to my parents, but for me, this is no normal rest. For six weeks, I pee and poop in my bed. I eat on that bed. I sleep in that bed. I watch TV in that bed. I study in that bed. The school has granted me leave, but I will have to take the final exams.

These are unbearable six weeks. During the day my parents have to go to work and Thatha has to do his own thing.

For the first time, I am all alone in the house. It feels like being in a haunted house. The real horror is having to listen to the sound of other kids playing outside in the evening, while I am stuck in bed. Eventually, though, Thatha bars the kids from playing downstairs because he notices that the pain of missing out is too much for me to handle.

The exile ends in a staggered manner. After six weeks, I am allowed to walk and resume attending school. But I am advised to avoid strenuous activity: no running for the next three months, and no cricket for the next six. Appa is so paranoid that he hides all the cricket bats, lest I pick one up and hurt myself again. My immediate worry, though, is something else. I no longer fit into my school uniforms.

Appa's earlier adventure with homoeopathy and self-medication might have brought an end to my wheezing episodes, but it is doing funny things to my body. Within the past six weeks, I have gone from 40 kg to 65 kg. To add to that, I am missing cricket. So I begin bunking classes to accompany the school team to matches and volunteer as a scorer. I must be involved in some way or another. I score the game in which Abhinav Mukund, three years my junior and a student at Vidya Mandir School, scores a hundred against us. I ask around about him; it turns out this is his first century in Under-10 cricket. It is the first of many because he is good. During the hot, boring afternoons, when nobody is watching, I turn our home into my field of dreams. I just stand out there in the courtyard and imagine myself playing entire Test matches. I get padded up, wear the team colour (blue when India are batting, yellow when it's Australia) and tie a handkerchief around my head because I don't have access to helmets yet, which are expensive. I imagine the entire field set, I imagine the bowler running in, and then I play the shot. And I provide commentary too.

Some of these matches are purely imaginary, some are improvisations on real-life games, but cricketing logic is always there. If Sachin has been getting out to the short ball from Glenn McGrath, in my matches, I set the field trap for the short ball and then make Sachin cut it up and over the point fielder. And I make the commentator say that with amazement. And if it is Sachin against Australia, my narration is always in an excited, histrionic voice, which is my impression of Tony Greig.

I play out the entire Chepauk Test of 1999 all over again in my house, only with a slight tweak. Instead of top-edging the pull, in the match orchestrated by me, Nayan Mongia flicks the ball safely for a single, and then India go on to win the Test. I usually play these matches when nobody is home, but I am so addicted that I sneak out for these games during my parents' Sunday afternoon naps. How is it possible that they don't notice that their son is up to something that can't be considered normal? Even I know it is not normal, which is why I keep it low-key. I am not sure if they are too tired to bother or if they have resigned themselves to living with a cricket maniac.

* * *

During bedrest, I develop a bond with the TV. For many hours each day, it is my only companion. Even when I study, I keep the TV on. I miss professional wrestling, which has for some reason gone off the air in India. I remember our wrestling matches on the terrace, with mattresses serving as the ring. I loved the high-flying moves. It is a miracle nobody got badly hurt. To keep my mind off everything I miss, I watch more TV.

Soon, I find myself unable to study or read without a background score. I just cannot read a book without TV, a song or whatever ambient noise. Both register in my ears.

This is when, on a Sunday, I watch an old Tamil movie, Sivaji Ganesan's *Motor Sundaram Pillai*, with Appa. I find it entertaining. When the bedrest is over but the cricket hasn't yet resumed, Appa takes me to the cinema halls for movies. He loves action movies centred on a larger-than-life policeman. He tells me he always wanted to be one, but Thatha didn't let him pursue that dream. This is why he feels a certain pride when constables salute him on the road. At least someone believes he could be a policeman.

Besides, these cop movies generally tell you to do the right thing. He takes me to other movies that I want to watch too, but that is in addition to these police dramas. Initially, I go to the movies for the popcorn and the soft drinks, but I am soon hooked. At times, we watch three to four movies a week. With newer movies, it is impossible to get a ticket in Madras cinema halls, but Appa never buys from the touts. Everything has to be proper and right. Many times, we return home and go another day. On one occasion, in 2000, I start crying because we are not getting tickets for Vijay's *Kushi*. This time, Appa gives in and buys from the tout at a premium.

For his son alone, Appa breaks the rules. I know because I have helped him make ledger calculations when he brings the books home on days when he is not in the office. Part of his job is to approve expenses and clear vendors' bills, which he refuses to do without proper authentication and ledger entries. In the past, he has seen all the bills get cleared without authentication on days when he is not around. Instead of confronting the culprits—he saves his confrontations for me—he just brings the books home whenever he is on leave.

On a cricket field, Appa's earnestness translates to doing anything to compete, but within the rules. He has no place for grey areas; do anything you can to win a game of cricket as long as you stay within the law. Once it's done, it's done and dusted, he tells me. He asks me to appeal louder. Always to greet the umpire to stay on side of him. Talk to him if he disagrees with your appeal, and tell him what you are trying to do with the ball. Convince him, but never fight with him.

Appa tells me what Kapil Dev did to Peter Kirsten was right: mankading him because he was leaving the crease too early at the non-striker's end. He also tells me of the time Courtney Walsh almost did it against Pakistan in the 1987 World Cup but stopped himself. That is why West Indies got knocked out, he tells me. Do not let batters get away with it, he says.

At twelve, I am bowling during a tense climax for Rao's Cricket Clinic, our PSBB school coach Chandrasekhar Rao's team, against DAV Gopalapuram at the RKM Cricket Ground, when I see Appa gesture from behind the striker that the non-striker is stealing ground even before I let the ball go. He wants me to mankad him.

I do it. No one thinks it's weird, and there are no protests. The coach just doesn't speak to Appa for a week.

Appa and Chandrasekhar Rao have a love–hate relationship. He is the only coach that Appa can take any liberties with because they fight and eventually make up. With others, he maintains distance and protocol. Sure enough, a year later, in an Under-14 match for Rao's Cricket Clinic against Prahlad Cricket Academy, I run out Anirudha Srikkanth in similar fashion. Anirudha is disgusted. He talks about it with others too. We argue it out as we often tend to, but this time Appa is not present for the coach to express his disapproval.

* * *

One rule that will not be broken is: no cricket until I heal fully. The doctor has told Appa that I need to be careful with stretching my left leg in the recovery period. When I bat right-handed, which is my natural style, the left leg is the leading leg. In order to avoid stretching the left leg, I convince Appa to let me go and play as a left-hand batter in street cricket. Slowly, I develop fully as a left-hand batter. I score a couple of half-centuries as a left-hand batter in weekend games. I can play every shot in the book left-handed except for the cut. I start bunking school and follow our school cricket team. I score for them, help out with advice, chuck balls at batters—anything to stay involved.

While the bats are hidden at home, there is an old wooden tennis racquet still available. When I am not playing cricket matches in my head in the afternoons, I am playing tennis against the courtyard wall. My favourite player is Andre Agassi, so the wall is always Pete Sampras. I hate Sampras because he hardly ever loses to Agassi. Not in my home. Here, I make Agassi win all the time.

I love playing other sports—I represented Tamil Nadu in ball-badminton during this cricket break, and I did so systematically and with utmost passion—but nothing matches the joy and emotion that cricket evokes in me. No other sport allows me the expression that cricket does. I can't find this happiness anywhere else. It just gives me so much joy and expression on the field. It has place for so many different people: people who don't want to think and just play the game. People with super skills can play the game without having to do anything and just express themselves. People with the utmost discipline and commitment can play this game. There is an opportunity for people who can actually innovate. There is skill, there is mental resolve, there is physical resolve, and you can take people on.

Sometimes just the opportunity to put twenty-two people together gives me a great kick. When it rains during school cricket games, I just hold on to the grilled gate of my house to see if it stops. Once, at the age of nine, I saw on TV that they tried to dry the pitch with a hair dryer in Cuttack during the 1996 Titan Cup. When it rained in Madras, I tried the same on our front-yard pitch, running out with Amma's hair dryer. The match in Cuttack couldn't be played; my efforts were met with similar failure in West Mambalam, but a wet pitch wasn't enough to stop us from playing.

* * *

There is another gate with bars, from which I look through longingly. It's on Alagiri Sami Salai in KK Nagar. Our school, PSBB, runs from one end of the street to the other. It is a huge campus with three gates: for KG students, for primary school and for secondary school. Where I stand, outside the school, is busy and chaotic before the classes start and end. The lane is converted into a one-way route during those hours. Shops selling stationery and sweets are crowded with students.

The first thing I see from outside is our pocket-sized cricket field. This is where our school practice happens. This is where our school had its first cricket tournament, sponsored by HLL. This is where I can't go because I cannot yet resume playing cricket.

Not being able to play makes me feel like an alien in school, which is otherwise a joyful place for us. I am back to doing things

I am not good at. I don't feel like I belong with a lot of the kids at school. Their lives, their pressures and their distractions are vastly different from mine. The only friends I have are the ones who turn up for the after-school basketball games.

In the classroom, I am an outsider whom the other kids try to instigate to do mischief. One day, when our teacher is absent and there is no substitute teacher in the class, out comes a jar of coconut oil that another boy has snuck into the school. No one has the courage to carry out the rest of the act. When it is presented to me that way by the boy—'I dared to bring the oil to school, now nobody has the guts to pour it on the blackboard'—I don't need a second invitation. If someone dares me to do something, then I have to do it. I am the centre of attention, I am doing something daring, why not?

I pour the oil all over the blackboard, rendering it useless for three days. For two of those three days, none of the forty students in the class gives me up to the principal, who has personally taken an interest in finding out who ruined the blackboard. Finally, one of us cracks, and I am suspended for a day, which I have to spend in the library.

At thirteen to fourteen years of age, in a co-ed school, we are a nuisance around the girls. We don't know what they like, but we want to impress them. For some reason, combing your hair properly is the consensus move to impress girls in the year 2000. Every boy carries a comb in his pocket, those small combs with a hole for the finger. Inevitably, they turn into toys for us. We stand in a triangle and play catch with them during the lunch break. There are three girls sitting behind us, having their lunch. One throw is so erratic that it hits the tube light, which breaks on one of the girls and into their lunch.

Evidently, they are not fans of shards of glass in their rice. They rush to the staff room, and off we go to the principal again. If it is Ashwin, they know whom to call: HLL. They know Amma because she arranges the HLL sponsorship for school tournaments and events. The other two boys' parents are not inconvenienced. All the ire is directed at me. In the presence of Amma, the principal—

anticipating some contrition—tells me in a grave tone that I have caused damage to school property.

'Ma'am, the tube light costs sixty-six rupees. We will pay twenty-two each.'

The principal loses it and sends me out of the room. Out of the classroom, out of the principal's office—if it were safe outside, I would be out of the school. Fifteen minutes later, Amma comes out and tells me they wanted to suspend me for a week and that she had to beg and plead with them to let me continue attending school.

I want to be everywhere, enjoy everything. I don't have a vote in SPL (Student People's Leader) elections—you vote only after passing out of ninth standard—but I campaign for my sports friends. I stand with placards and sloganeer. There is nothing I won't do to entertain myself.

Except when this girl with a beaming smile, Prithi, joins our Hindi class in the eighth standard, I can't immediately summon the courage to go talk to her. I am tall, and she is tall, so we sit next to each other somewhere in the back rows. She has an alluring personality, which makes her popular. She is always surrounded by friends. As it happens in Class Eight, I am attracted to her. Almost at first sight. And as it happens in Class Eight, I can't find a way to express it. As it happens in our schools, it becomes a scandal. The tragedy of it is that the rest of the class knows I like her, which means she has become the centre of unwanted attention. I think she hates me for that.

One fine day, she finds my name scribbled on her Hindi notebook. And she has also started getting blank calls at home. She feels she has become part of some big scandal, with the boy not even approaching her. She brings the notebook art to the attention of a teacher and thus begins another investigation whose prime suspect is R. Ashwin. Prithi is a favourite of the teacher who happens to be in charge of this case. This is an open-and-shut case as far as everyone else is concerned.

I know what's brewing, so I cook up an illness and avoid school for a couple of days, but you can't stay away forever. When I finally do make it to school, this teacher nabs me. She sends the whole class out and calls two other teachers for interrogation.

Thoughts are running through my head at ten per second as the class empties out.

'What if my parents are called?'

'I can prove my innocence by getting call logs, but how the hell will I ask my parents for those logs? What does a fourteen-year-old need phone records for?'

'Why didn't Prithi confront me instead of going to the teachers?'

'Is she being bullied by others because they know I like her, and now my name has appeared on her notebook?'

As my friend Adithya, who sits next to me, gets up to leave, I tell him, like a murder accused being sent to the gallows, I am innocent.

'*Machan*, I didn't do this *ra*.'

His parting words are to the effect of: If you don't confess and fail to convince these teachers of your innocence, it will get really tricky, and they will involve the principal too.

But I go on to tell the judicial panel that my handwriting is ugly, there is no way I write my name this well. I offer to take a live handwriting test, but these teachers are made of sterner stuff. Or they think I am made of sterner stuff.

'You can forge your handwriting in front of us. Bring us your notebooks, and we will match the handwriting from there.'

After minutes of rummaging through various notebooks—as if I am a professional criminal who can go to the extent of producing fake notebooks here—they are satisfied it is not me who has written my name on Prithi's Hindi notebook. Of course, it doesn't strike their minds that I could have changed my handwriting when writing my scandalous name on Prithi's notebook.

Emboldened by this mini breakthrough, I ask them if Prithi's parents have caller ID at home. It is a device that shows you the number of the caller. She says no. 'Ah ha.' How can she say it's me if she doesn't have caller ID?

With my name cleared and my honour restored, I find the courage to approach her in a quietly dramatic fashion. Instead of talking to Prithi during school hours, I find out there is a boy who gets off the bus outside the same apartment building as her. I ask him for her flat number. Then I call 197—telephone enquiry—

to find out her phone number, and then make an unsolicited call to her. To tell her it wasn't me who made the earlier unsolicited calls. To tell her it wasn't me who wrote in her notebook. To tell her I like her.

For the next two years, we have flowing conversations on the phone, but we hardly talk to each other when in class. She thinks I am a bit of a loafer because she hardly sees me in school. My cricket has resumed, and I disappear for days. Two years later, we go to different schools. And the phone calls gradually stop.

* * *

When I am finally back playing cricket, I am asked to stay away from bowling lest I injure myself again. On one of the Sundays, even Amma gives up her rest day and comes to watch me play. At the end of the day she asks me, 'Why do you just keep standing in the field all day? Why don't you do something?'

'Amma, I bat. I will injure myself again if I bowl fast.'

'Yes, batting and all is great, but what is the point of standing there all by yourself all day? Do something. Experiment. Bowl some legspin.'

Immediately, Appa intervenes and shows off his technical expertise, saying legspin is not easy. Appa is right. Legspinners impart the turn primarily through the wrist. The ball turns away from a right-hand batter. It is difficult to master and replicate the release every time, which creates room for error. Few legspinners do well in Test cricket.

'Is it?' goes Amma. 'Okay, bowl offspin then.'

Off-spin bowling is indeed easier than legspin. Offspinners impart spin primarily through the fingers. There is much better control over the release. However, unlike legspinners, who can make the ball turn the other way by releasing the ball from the back of the hand, offspinners don't have too many toys. Their strength is accuracy, which tends to work in Tests, but I want to turn the ball the other way too.

'You go to the ground and stay out all day. It is like me going to office. I do something all day. If you get out first ball, you need to do something else. You can't just stand there all day and clap for others. What is the point of playing the game then?'

So, I start working on bowling offspin part-time, but my immediate challenge is not to find the deception I want. People have started telling me I have become slow. I have never been flash on the field—even when I was 25 kg lighter—but I have never had issues moving around the field. I was actually a good fielder because I have good hands. Even at the age of eight or nine, I wasn't afraid of high catches. Now, though, people have a reason to target me. I am still batting and catching well, but there is a tag I carry now.

The tag makes it easier to exclude me if somebody else 'has to' get into a team. Selection in junior categories when nobody but the selectors are watching is trickier than at the more prominent levels. At each age level—Under-13, 15 and 17—in Tamil Nadu, an inter-district tournament is conducted. The competition in Madras is more intense. Each year, about 500–600 of the best boys in Madras are invited to the nets. The selectors are watching many of them for the first time. In three days, they have to prune the list down to about sixty for a four-team tournament to identify Madras's team for the inter-district tourney.

I keep scoring runs there, but in the first year since the injury, I am told I have played hardly any cricket. The next year, my fitness is brought up. Every time my batting is spoken about, someone talks about me being slow on the park. And no one tells me this officially. I just have to ask the people locally, and they tell me what they hear. Even when I make it to the newspaper articles, the last paragraph makes a reference to my waistline, pointing out that I need to shed weight to make it to the next level. However, no one really tells me what I need to do to get quicker and lighter.

Every time I read or hear that line, I punish myself more. It is a dare. Like someone telling me I don't have the guts to spill coconut oil on the blackboard. So I run and run and run. It is a daunting task to go to a coach or a selector and tell him I am not losing weight, no matter how hard I work. I don't have the wherewithal to work smart, but I have the mental and physical resolve. I step on the weighing machine every day, and if it hasn't reduced by 500 grams, I make a change to my training and lifestyle.

Every day, I make a change. If I have been running 10 laps, I make it 12. I keep reducing the amount of food I eat, one spoonful at a time, and walking longer after meals. The body is young; it takes it all without revolting.

Yuvraj Singh makes a sensational debut in the Champions Trophy in 2000. In his interviews, he talks about how much milk he drinks. So, I start drinking a lot of milk, which makes me feel bloated. I later discover that I am lactose-intolerant.

I have become really good at running long distances because I can keep pushing myself even when my body is ready to give up. Whenever I try to sprint, though, it seems like I am running on a treadmill: a lot of effort but little movement. Because of that hip injury, my upper body and lower body are not in sync. I am unable to punch through with the lower body; it is all just the upper body and arms. Even when I think I am successful at sprinting, I am not really going that fast because the upper body and the lower body are working in their own different ways. There is a lot of effort and exhaustion, but it doesn't translate into speed on the park. Nor does the needle on the weighing scale budge. Others eat more and work less than me, but are in much better shape.

Appa manages to find a way again. He finds me an athletic trainer, which means a momentary pause in the cricket I play in 1st Street, Ramakrishnapuram. This trainer shows me how to work smart, which muscles to work on, and what kind of workouts will help me lose weight and gain speed. I am not a mad bull anymore, running here and there without any results.

This is what my day looks like now. Appa drops me off at cricket practice early in the morning. He goes back home, gets ready for work—proper bush shirt, trousers, polished boots, aviators, et al.—and carries my breakfast and my school uniform. When I am fed and dressed, he drops me off at school. Thatha is there with his bicycle and his gunny-sack carrier to pick me up from school and take me to the YMCA, where I work with the athletic trainer from 4.45 p.m. to 5.30 p.m.

Appa picks me up from the YMCA and takes me to the math tuition—private classes to supplement school education. I don't know what he does for the next hour, but when the class ends, he is there to take me to the next class. It is 10 p.m. by the time we get back home, his crisp clothes soft with sweat, me exhausted and riding pillion on his motorbike. Kangaroo and Joey, but unlike their nocturnal nature, we're looking for food and rest for the night before starting at dawn again.

* * *

Cow dung. Water. Small pebbles. Mud. Stumps.

That's what Amma and Appa think is needed to make cricket pitches. While watching one of the many cricket matches that Appa subjects the whole family to, Amma asks him why her son is playing on matting pitches when in international cricket he will be playing on different pitches. She asks Appa what those pitches are made of. Appa himself is a tennis-ball or matting-pitch cricketer, so he is not quite sure. So, he guesses.

After my Class Ten board exams, we have a three-month break. I use all the knowledge gleaned from my parents' conversations to make a thick mixture out of cow dung, water and mud. Sometimes, Amma helps too. The 10th Sector Ground has a hard patch that could be turned into a cricket pitch. I pour the mixture all over the patch and roll it with a stump. I use a big slab to flatten it, doing what a roller does. In some places, I throw in small, fine stones to make the ball turn. Hari, my next-door neighbour, is my accomplice for some of the time. We leave it overnight because the next morning we are playing a Test match.

Through some magic and sheer love of the game, by 5 a.m., all twenty-two cricketers—all schoolboys—have made it to the sector ground on their bicycles. This ground is basically a public park but has very little grass. It works perfectly for us because it means fewer people come here for purposes other than 'Test' cricket. We are set for a Test match over five days. Play starts at 5.30 a.m. and ends at 10.30 a.m. It involves a Rasna break and a breakfast break, which would be whatever street food the cart is selling. We play with the 4Aces ball, a tennis ball especially made for cricket; it travels farther than the real tennis ball. In the first session, we tape the ball to replicate swinging conditions. In the second, we take off one side of the tape. In the final session, the ball is bare and pebbles are sprinkled to make it turn. The last session is only one hour long because it gets too hot.

When we don't have enough numbers for Test matches, we put together one team and go around looking for 14-over matches. These matches involve bets. Often, we all pool in Rs 10 each and put it on the line against the other team. Sometimes—especially if we are starting out with a new ball—we play for those 4Aces. We usually have more than eleven players, but not enough to play a Test match among ourselves. So, we keep using rolling substitutes in bet matches. Numbers always help because bet matches invariably end in fights.

Tennis-ball cricket is a massive phenomenon in Madras. During the summer break, you can't pass through a neighbourhood without witnessing at least one intense match going on in the sector ground. You don't need a proper turf, a pitch or equipment for these games. It is a pure expression of love for the game and competition.

Appa has played a lot of tennis-ball cricket in his day. He used to swing the tennis ball, which is an incredible skill. He shows me how to bowl the leg cutter where you run your fingers down the side of the ball. This way, the ball moves away from the right-hand batter after pitching.

Somasundaram Ground in T. Nagar is the hub of tennis-ball cricket. Tens of matches take place at the same time. All 14 overs a side. Everywhere you look, you will see a boy—mostly with a kerchief around his face—hurling down a tennis ball as fast or as craftily as he can. The batter's first instinct is to try to hit the biggest six he can. This is *the* sight in Madras during the summer holidays. It is so hot that many of us wear socks inside socks to keep our feet from burning. The heat and the dust is probably why the kerchief on the face.

My good friend Bhuvnesh is a serious tennis-ball player. His team plays in tournaments or bets on matches for big money. I am a bit of a gun for hire for these games. They pay me Rs 50 or Rs 100 to play for them. Apart from batting, I have the skills to bowl with a tennis ball. I can bowl the yorker, and I can run my fingers on the ball to bowl cutters. Bhuvnesh and his team don't think I am slow.

It is during one of these games that I come across SK. He has a beautiful and correct offspinner's action, but the ball turns in weird directions and zips off the dusty surfaces. All you see when he is bowling is the dust flying under the bat and the ball passing miles away from it. He bowls like an offspinner, but manages to turn it away too. When I go to bat against him, the first ball pitches in the sand and just zips off. I don't know what has just happened. I try to sweep the next ball, but the ball turns the other way. I then try the reverse sweep, but this time it turns normally and beats me again. I then step out to try to hit him, and the ball goes straight up off my bat for a catch to the wicketkeeper.

I ask around about him. He is a bit of a terror in these matches. I am completely fascinated by what he does with the ball. So I start shadowing him. I take my bike and ride to wherever he is playing. Everywhere he goes, he is unplayable. The tennis ball obeys his commands. It drops on the batter; it turns either way. For an offspinner to turn the ball the other way to the extent that he does, you have to chuck, which means bending and straightening the arm to a degree considered illegal in cricket. SK, though, doesn't look like he chucks.

I finally approach him to ask him how he does it. He is nice enough to show me that he flicks it with the middle finger and sends it out of the front of his hand when he wants to turn it the other way. I start working on it. It is not that difficult because the tennis ball is soft and almost gets squeezed at a touch. It comes out of the hand almost distorted. It does all sorts of tricks in the air.

In Madras, it is called the *sodakku* ball because of the click sound the thumb and middle finger make. I start bowling it in our tennis-ball matches as a change-up in my pace bowling. I run in with the ball covered in my left hand before transferring it to my right in the delivery stride so that the batter can't pick what I am bowling.

It brings me a lot of success, but I don't think even I or anyone else can do it with the hard cricket ball. That is, until the

Young Stars Cricket Association (YSCA) 30-overs tournament in Madras. It also coincides with a spin camp headed by former India legspinner V.V. Kumar at MAC B ground. I am at the camp. There is a rope going across the width of the pitch, and we are learning to bowl above it and get the ball to drop just after crossing it.

A team from Sri Lanka, which happens to be playing in the YSCA tournament, is also training at the same ground. Their coach recognizes V.V. Kumar and brings a kid from their team to introduce him to V.V. He agrees to watch the kid bowl and give his evaluation. Incredibly, this kid is bowling the *sodakku* with the hard cricket ball, besides a host of other deliveries. V.V. Kumar tells him to develop and master a stock ball first, and then try all the other variations.

* * *

Parle G is sponsoring an Under-16 schoolboys' tournament across the country. They have identified ten cities, which enter a team formed of their best schoolboy cricketers. It will culminate with a combined squad of fifteen selected from all the teams getting to spend a training camp with Mohinder Amarnath and Maninder Singh.

This takes me back to the Chinnaswamy Stadium dormitory. It has improved from six years ago, when we were basically sharing shop-like structures under the stands, but we still have to share the squatting-style toilets. All the teams are staying in the dormitory. The bathroom queues in the morning are understandably long. However, the boys from Delhi and Punjab are in a parallel queue. While we are waiting for our turn at the toilet, they are lining up to use the washbasins. It leaves us intrigued. And suspicious.

They are taking longer than it does to brush your teeth. For a while, it distracts us from our pressing need to make it to the toilet. A couple of us switch the queue, curious to find out what exactly is happening at the sinks. It turns out they are trimming their facial hair.

We look at each other's faces and see no hair. Our first reaction, as it is with competitive cricketers, is that there is no way these boys are under the age of sixteen. That's the first thing anyone from Madras with any experience of playing outside Madras tells us: the boys from the north are older than what they state.

And then you meet these boys. I make it to the probables but not the final camp. During the couple of days that I spend with the camp before I am sent home, I see these boys respond and react to Mohinder and Maninder. They are strongly built, their arms are huge, they are intimidating, and they have facial hair too, but they react and behave just like me. I go back wondering if boys from various parts of India are differently gifted physically. I find myself more interested in India's history, looking for those books in the library.

While I use the three-month break after the tenth board exams to roll pitches and play 'Test' matches with my friends, Appa takes me for an admission interview at St Bede's School, better known for its sports than PSBB. It is also a completely different school. PSBB is all hustle and bustle, full of energy and activity. St Bede's is quiet, next to the popular Santhome Church, almost on the beach. Classes have only two sections—A and B. PSBB could go up to J. The campus here is huge, but the buildings are fewer. The ceilings are higher, but not as high as the trees that surround them. I have scored good marks in the board exams, so I get in fairly easily.

There is still time before the school resumes, though. The trainer I work with also works at St Bede's, apart from the YMCA. So, I ask if we can train at St Bede's instead of the YMCA, even though the latter is much closer to home. He agrees. Thatha and I now take the 12B bus from near our home to Marina Beach, after which we walk 2 km to the school playground, which is on the opposite side of the beach and the school. After I complete my running around, I wait for S. Sharath to turn up, the real reason for my choosing to train at St Bede's.

Sharath is a hugely prolific Tamil Nadu batter. All of Madras believes he deserves to play for India but is unfairly kept out. He keeps scoring runs after runs for Tamil Nadu but cannot make it to international cricket. He is thirty now. He lives nearby and comes to St Bede's every evening to have a knock. He shows up with just his gloves on and his bat. He wants only gentle knocking, full tosses that he can hit back to get his bat swing right.

This is Tamil Nadu cricket in front of my eyes. I go and volunteer, 'Sharath sir, can I throw balls at you?' He agrees. Every ball comes back at a different speed. I have not seen a batter hit the ball this hard. He bats for thirty to forty minutes, and I throw balls at him in awe.

The cricket in-charge at St Bede's is a man named R.I. Palani. He is not a coach, but if you are a young cricketer in Madras, there is no way you haven't heard of him. He is an important person because he runs a lot of cricket operations in the Tamil Nadu Cricket Association (TNCA) leagues, which are contested in five divisions based on the quality of the teams owned by various corporate houses. These leagues are the supply chain not only for the highest level of cricket in Tamil Nadu but also for other states which send their 'guest players' here for exposure.

For any cricketer with serious ambitions, it is important to play in the first division. Most of the others who play with us have made it to first-division teams. Only my friend Santosh and I are left behind. We go on a desperate run of selection trials. I end up with an offer from Mambalam Mosquitoes, but Santosh doesn't have any.

Because he is in charge of our school cricket team, we decide to run this situation by Palani. He suggests we continue playing for Galaxy in the third division. Santosh goes on to pick around 40 wickets, I score around 700 runs, and we carry our team into the second division, which actually gets us noticed more than first division would have.

* * *

There's a movie called *12B*, based on the bus route I take every day. The film's director, Jeeva, used to take the same bus during his college days. The male lead of the film, played by the debuting Shaam, short for Shamshuddin Ibrahim—most Tamil movie stars are known by just one name, which is usually a nickname, suggesting their familiarity with the crowds—misses the 12B bus as he is distracted by one of the female leads of the movie, played by Jyothika. Our hero then gets mugged and loses his job. There is also a parallel track that depicts life if he had made it to the bus that morning.

For us, life is more prosaic. If we miss that 3.40 p.m. 12B from T. Nagar—I have started travelling alone from my home to T. Nagar, where Santosh is waiting for me—we will not get seats, as it starts getting crowded from 3.48 p.m. onwards. Let alone sitting, even entering the bus with our huge kitbags will be a task.

The drivers are helpful and wait for us to board the bus with our kitbags, but the conductors are ruthless. When they see our school pass, which allows us free rides from home to school and back, it is almost as if it is a loss to their personal treasury. They make sure to charge us for the kitbags. When we protest, we are told that fruit, vegetable and flower vendors also pay for their baskets.

We don't miss a chance to rile them up when we are in our school uniform during the day. When I am asked for the pass, I point to my school uniform and ask, 'Do you think I am an office-going person who has purposely dressed in school uniform to save on bus fare?'

The conductor is immovable. 'Who knows? I will only know if you have the pass.'

This year is especially tricky as there is a typographical error in my name's spelling on the pass and the photo is a little dated. Bus conductors usually don't have the time to bother with verifying the pass, but there are always the eccentric ones.

'Is this you?' this one asks me, looking at the photo.

'Yes sir.'

'What is your name? A-s-u-r-a-n? Asuran? Show me any of your books. I will check the label.'

I take out a book.

'What name is this?' he asks, pointing at the book.

'Ashwin, sir.'

He then shows me the pass. 'What is written here?'

'Asuran, sir, but that is a mistake made by your office only. They must have misread it.'

'No, no, I will not allow you on the bus. Either give me the fare or get off at the next stop.'

I get down and have to take the next bus. Unlike in the movie, there are no dramatic changes in my life because I miss this particular bus. Movies, though, are an inseparable part of life in Madras. This could well be a parallel comedy track that runs in most

Tamil movies. It has nothing to do with the main plot, but Tamil movies can't survive without this humour. The great comedian Goundamani doesn't need to be the friend or sidekick of the hero. He is not a slave to the storyline either. He is there with his sidekick, Senthil, running their own comedy in the middle of a serious film. The movies can do without the hero, but not without this humour.

Tamil is an inherently humorous language. The range of expression is huge. What a word means depends on the tone it is spoken in, which in turn can depend on whom it is spoken to, how hot the day is, how busy the streets are.

And the streets are never not busy. Madras lives its life in the streets. We do too. If it is not official league cricket or our 'Test' matches or matches for Bhuvnesh's team for cash—sometimes up to Rs 500—it is the cricket in our street at 4 p.m.

Appa doesn't want me to play this cricket because coaches have told him it will ruin my game. He comes up with errands or school assignments precisely at that time. I see through it and I tell him I will only bowl and field and not bat because it is the batting that he is most concerned about. It is not that easy to convince him, though. Even if he lets me go, he watches from the balcony. Only when he leaves do I get to bat. Mostly, though, he is watching.

I enjoy whatever batting I manage to get in. There are so many constraints that you have to innovate. My pull is getting better in trying to avoid the windows straight behind the bowler. Because the bigger boys chuck in fast and straight to try to hit your leg three times and get you out, I have learned to get my feet out of the way and drive balls to off.

I yearn to make everything competitive. I have started getting the guys to bring a rupee or two each and bet on these games. I figure if there is something at stake, they will take it more seriously. I even badmouth the bigger boys when I hit them. Just so that they come back hard at me and I don't have to play a non-competitive match.

I start innovating with rules to make it more competitive. Not all of them make sense. If the ball goes out on the full, you are out, but if it hits the next house's wall and comes back in, you have hit a six. So if you take the risk, you hit it hard enough to give it a chance to come back into the field of play off the wall. If the ball touches a fielder on the way out, you can't be out. If the ball bounces on the ground and then goes out, we have fielders in place, and the batters have to run their runs.

There is another reason Appa doesn't want me playing in the streets. He fears everything. That I'll get hit by a bike or a car. He keeps telling me that even the smallest injury can put an end to my cricket career. When he restrains me inside, I find my cousin and start playing inside. He is strong and athletic, and we play indoors with a hard cricket ball and still miraculously do not break anything. I don't know how we get away with it, especially with the TV so close to our wicket. One day, we are playing football on the terrace. The next day, I have a serious cricket match. I am trying to score a goal, and he stomps on my foot. To avoid letting Appa know, I immediately limp my way to sleep. In the morning, my foot has swollen up like a blowfish. I put on three socks, thinking it will help me cover it up, but Appa knows as soon as he sees me walk.

I still go on to play the match, field for 30 overs, don't bowl and score 30-odd runs. Then come back and play in the street. Selection doesn't matter here. Your weight doesn't matter here. Only your competitiveness.

On most days, after we finish cricket, we end up at Muthu's soup stall outside a famous supermarket in our neighbourhood. Muthu is from Pudukkottai, a town seven hours from Madras. He sells plantain soup, tomato soup, vegetable soup, French onion soup and cabbage soup. If we want a different variety, though, he makes it for us and brings it the next day. He indulges us. He talks to us, takes an interest in our cricket, and we take over his stall for at least an hour every day.

Muthu has colourful plastic stools for customers to sit on. We grab all of them, form a circle and chat away while we polish off fifteen to twenty portions of soup every time we go there. Anyone who has to go to Muthu for soup has to go past our circle.

We often see his brother sitting there with not much work to do. So, like the larger-than-life hero in Tamil movies who can solve problems with one swing of an invisible magic wand, I offer him money if he wants to set up another stall elsewhere for his brother. Muthu doesn't want a loan. He politely tells us our patronage is enough help for him.

We are not blessed with the subtlety of Muthu. On one particularly hot afternoon, as I peer out of the window, waiting for it to be 4 p.m. so we can play, I see a boy lying down on our pitch, bare-chested but wearing shorts and pads. We don't let outsiders come in to play on our patch, so I am intrigued by who the boy is.

I quickly go down and immediately recognize the boy. He is one of our regular players, but I can't remember his name immediately because he has changed it around eight times already because of numerology or something. All the time, he talks of his dream of playing for India. He is a decent cricketer, slightly better with the cricket ball than the tennis ball in the street. He has good ball sense.

But I am questioning his overall sense as I see a thick red fluid on his bicep. I run back into the house to quickly call up Bhuvnesh and the others. They come riding on their bicycles as fast as they can. With strength in numbers, I finally draw up the courage to find out what has happened to him.

He has broken a Ruchi pickle bottle and used the glass to write 'India' in blood on his bicep.

'What's wrong with you?' we ask him.

'I want to play for India. I want India to know how much I want it. If I have to hurt myself to earn it, I am ready to do it.'

We are concerned but are also looking at each other's faces, hoping someone else is the first one to laugh and ask for the treat that is customary among us whenever someone gets hurt. Sai, one of our players, finds the broken pickle bottle, brings another piece of glass and offers to write 'South Africa' and 'Australia' too. Just to cast the net wider. 'If you have written India, they pick only fifteen. This way, you will have a better chance of getting selected.'

Indeed, they pick only fifteen.

4

It is not daylight yet as I look out of my window. We are on the Dadar Express to Bombay, but Appa has woken me up well before our destination. The train has been stationary for a while near Lonavala. He is picking up all our stuff even as my eyes adjust to the dim light. The train is scheduled to reach Dadar by 6 a.m., but we are still about 150 km away and are certain to be late. Our destination, as usual, is Wankhede Stadium, but not for a Test match this time. I have to report for my India Under-17 selection trials, which I will miss at this rate.

All those years ago, Appa traded his dreams for the job security provided by the Indian Railways, also his father's employer. Ironically, now, a tardily running Indian Railways train is in the way of his son's, and I suspect his own renewed, dream. He sheds his middle-class inhibitions and musters up the courage and the money to get us a private taxi to Thane. But we're not taking the taxi all the way into Mumbai, retaining some of our austerity. Thane is a suburb just outside the city, and Appa knows we can get on a local train from there.

We make it in time to report at the camp, but I am already regretting not taking up Thatha's many offers to teach me Hindi. I can read and write Hindi, but the Hindi spoken in the world outside Tamil Nadu is nowhere close to what we are taught in textbooks. I have been cracking Hindi exams in school by using the old trick of flicking half the words from the question. If the question is, Who was India's first prime minister? I don't necessarily need to know the exact spelling of 'pradhan mantri'. I can copy that from the question.

At the camp, though, the first question I am asked is, 'Naam kya hai?' It literally translates to: 'what is name?' I am not prepared for this kind of colloquial, informal Hindi. For seconds I am trying to figure out whose name the peon wants to know. Then I translate it to Tamil in my head and realize that even in colloquial Tamil they ask you 'peyar enna?' and not 'unkal peyar enna?'

So I cut short my rote answer from 'mera naam Ashwin hai' to 'Ashwin'. I am taken to the spot where forty to forty-five of us are completing the formalities. Then we are each handed an envelope with our daily allowances and our room number at the nearby Sea Green hotel. The allowance is Rs 300 per day, and five of us have to share one hotel room. Luckily, there are two other boys in my room whose first language is not Hindi. One of them is Abhishek Hegde from Kerala, a funny, stockily built guy.

The other boy is Anirudha Srikkanth. Of all the hotels in the world, of all the rooms in the hotel, it had to be the one with Anirudha, my long-time friend, nemesis, at times my opening partner, mankading victim and often my captain, with whose career mine has been intertwined right from our Under-14 days. We have both been opening batters, we have both scored heavily for our schools and Tamil Nadu age-group teams, but he has more games against Goa than I have.

In fact, the first time I got to face Goa, the weakest team in the South Zone, was during my third tournament for the Tamil Nadu state team, just before coming here. They had no choice this time. In the game before the Goa one, Anirudha and I opened the innings against a strong Hyderabad side. I should have been duck-out, but I was dropped in the slips. Then I was involved in Anirudha getting run out for a duck. I went on to score a double-century, followed by runs throughout the tournament. Anirudha ended up losing his place in the side towards the end of the tournament.

Here we are again, in the same hotel room, fighting for the same spot. We have all heard of the unofficial quota system well before arriving. Only one boy from Tamil Nadu gets selected for the Indian teams. That's true across all age groups. Uttar Pradesh gets three almost every time. Bombay is often well-represented.

One of the two kids we have heard the most about in the camp is Rohit Sharma, who comes with a bat with an old green SG sticker. We have heard that he is the future. We have heard how he travels with his kitbag on the crowded local trains.

The other is Cheteshwar Pujara, who is only 15 and has already scored a triple-century in Under-14 cricket. This year he has scored a double-century in the Under-17 West Zone matches for Saurashtra. There is an aura around him, an aura of thousands of runs.

* * *

This is as far as Appa can join me. He needs to resume work. He also doesn't have a place to stay in Bombay.

On the first two days, we bat and bowl in the nets before we are split for selection matches among ourselves. V. Chamundeswaranath is the selector from the South Zone. He played first-class cricket for Andhra and is an influential functionary in cricket circles. The man making the final call, though, will be India's chief selector for Under-17 teams, Pravin Amre, who has played cricket with distinction for India.

As we go about our business in the nets, I spot the legendary Dilip Vengsarkar talking to Anirudha, who is not just an aspiring cricketer but the son of his former teammate and friend, Kris Srikkanth. Vengsarkar is a towering figure, and he spends the rest of his stay talking to Amre and watching us play.

In the evening, I walk to the hotel alone. This is the first time I am out of the south on my own. Everywhere I look, I see big, intimidating restaurants. I walk past Not Just Jazz By The Bay, where a bunch of kids, who look my age, are waiting for a table. It looks like an upscale restaurant, the kind they show in Hollywood films. These kids look like they belong there. I imagine I am sticking out in my cricket kit, unable to speak the language on the street. I'm not looking forward to going back to a room where we aren't exactly friendly. Outside the room, we haven't been introduced to the forty or so other boys at the camp. Nobody knows Who's Who.

I can't imagine walking into Not Just Jazz By The Bay. Or any other restaurant. They are all intimidating and, I imagine, expensive. What if I end up eating something I can't pay for? I spot a blue cart carrying street food and settle for aloo chat, which is deep-fried potatoes with spices sprinkled on top, for dinner. As I eat, I replay in my head Anirudha talking to Dilip Vengsarkar and assume he will be the one boy who gets selected from Tamil Nadu.

After two days of nets, we are split into teams for two days of selection matches. My team loses the toss, and we are asked to bat first. For many of us, this is our first experience of playing at Wankhede, and it is everything we have heard of. Early in the morning, on the fresh pitch, there is extravagant bounce and movement off the surface for the bowlers. Umesh Karvi from Karnataka, against whom I have played previously in the South Zone, is letting it rip and has us down at 27 for 5 in no time. I walk in and score 40 odd runs. It gets easier to bat in the afternoon. It's the same story the next day, when we lose the toss again and struggle in difficult conditions to bat.

The next morning, we are asked to assemble at the place where we first registered ourselves. A peon is announcing the names of the fifteen players selected to play Under-17 cricket for India. This is the dream, the stepping stone for an international career. I have made all the calculations in my mind. Only one from me and Anirudha will be selected. The names will be read out alphabetically. My official name is Ravichandran Ashwin and his is Anirudha Srikkanth so I am bracing for Anirudha's name to come up in the first few and put me out of my misery. Anirudha is standing right next to me. They move past A without naming him.

It is an excruciating process, although it doesn't take more than two minutes in all. Now my mind has changed the calculation. I am thinking that he probably goes by Srikkanth Anirudha, which means our names are next to each other. Ten names have gone by, and neither of us has been selected yet. I am still watching out for a call for Anirudha and don't even answer the call for 'Ravichandran Ashwin'. They call my name again, and I realize I am officially an India Under-17 player. I will have a blue jersey of my own now.

A.G. Pradeep from Andhra is our captain. Uday Kaul from Punjab is the wicketkeeper. I am the only one from Tamil Nadu. There are exactly three boys from Uttar Pradesh: vice-captain Ravikant Shukla, all-rounder Ali Murtaza and legspinner Piyush Chawla. Rohit Sharma makes it. Cheteshwar Pujara doesn't.

Even before I can process what's happened, we are instructed to pack our stuff from Sea Green and move to the Garware Pavilion at Wankhede Stadium. Our new daily allowance envelopes carry Rs 1000 per day. Automatically, we assume a different air: we are now in rooms shared by two and have more money in our pockets while the others are going home. What makes this extra special for me is that Pravin Amre has stuck his neck out for me and overruled the other selectors because I batted in both of the morning sessions and actually scored some runs. This is what we had heard about Bombay: tough runs are valued there.

* * *

I have it all planned out now. I am the only opener in the squad. I am going to score a lot of runs in this Asia Cup and get selected for the senior international team. I will put on that blue jersey, puff my chest out as the national anthem plays, look at the India flag with pride, and give my blood and sweat for the team. Pretty soon, Tony Greig will actually commentate in matches where I bat with Sachin Tendulkar. He will marvel at how good this new partner of the Little Master is. I will take on the rare bowler who troubles him; we will knock gloves in the middle of the pitch when I hit a boundary, and he will nod at me, but I have not imagined what he will tell me, or what language he will use. I have not imagined what I will do if someone knows neither Tamil nor English.

At the India Under-17 camp in Bombay, they speak anything but Tamil and English. That 'anything' is just various dialects of Hindi. The only person who speaks English in this camp is

Piyush Chawla. Everybody else just assumes everyone knows Hindi and sets off speaking their own version of Hindi. I find it rude and alienating that no one makes an effort to talk to the one boy who doesn't know their language. I make an effort to talk, but by the time I process what is being said and translate my Tamil response into bookish Hindi, they have moved on. All that is legible to me is their laughter. All I can make out is that they are making fun of me, but I don't know what exactly is being said. If they speak Hindi as it is written in textbooks, I might still understand it, but this is completely different. I feel left out, humiliated and intimidated.

Our coach, Venkatesh Prasad, whose celebrations we have grown up imitating, speaks only Hindi. He is from Karnataka; his Hindi can't be great, but from whatever he says, even he sounds like a scholar of Hindi to me. He has only just retired from cricket and is starting out on a coaching career. He makes sure that everybody comes together and has meals at the same time. He takes us on educational trips. He takes us to an airfield, then to meet underprivileged kids to sensitize us, but I wonder why he can't see a boy as uncomfortable and out of place as I am in this camp. Even my roommate, A.G. Pradeep from Andhra, speaks only Hindi during the camp. As a result, I can't wait for the matches to begin.

In the nets, Prasad asks me to focus more on my offspin bowling than my batting, even though I am the only one in the whole squad who has opened regularly for his state. The day finally arrives when I don the India jersey at the Chinnaswamy Stadium in Bangalore against Nepal. I am expecting to open, but that role is given to Uday Kual and Ali Murtaza. I am sent out to bat at No. 6. Most cricketers wear spiked shoes when batting or bowling to avoid slipping, but I am not very fond of them or other accessories. I am not yet comfortable wearing helmets either. I wear spikes when bowling but bat in flats. I score only 4, bowl four economical overs and am dropped for Rohit Sharma in the next match. The national anthem wasn't even played.

Throughout the rest of the tournament, no one tells me why I am not being played. Even if I want to ask the reason, whom do I ask and in what language? All Prasad asks me is why I didn't wear spikes when batting. Not that it resulted in a run-out or anything. Surely that is not being held against me? Surely they are not judging me based on how amateurish I am with the equipment I use?

Even as India keep winning in the league stages, my focus moves on to my studies. Pretty soon, I have to take my Class XII board exams, and I am the only one carrying books. Board exams are a big event in any student's life. This is the time when the education board pushes you out of your comfort zone. You don't write the exam in your own school; you are not supposed to identify yourself on the answer paper; you are just a roll number, and then your answer sheets are sent for evaluation to randomly selected teachers. Every effort is made to make this a universally comparable score across India. Except that the practical exams take place in your own school and account for 25 per cent of the score. These are your home matches.

I have already forfeited these home matches for my cricket. Appa has obtained special permission for me to miss the practical exams, but he has been told that while the school will let me write the exams without attending these practicals, I will have to do without these marks. It just means I need to work harder for the written exams. Whenever I sit down to study, though, it is as if that makes me the biggest loser in the world. The other players taunt me for studying and run around shouting, 'Yeh padh raha hai, yeh padh raha hai'. Then the others come and ask me questions which I don't understand because of the heavy usage of Hindi, and then they laugh among themselves.

Eventually, I start to go to the bathroom, the only place where I can find some quiet, lay in the bathtub, and study there for hours on end. One day one of the players comes and starts banging on the door. Even before I can come out, he runs out shouting something in Hindi. The next day everybody asks me what I was up to in the bathroom. When I tell them I was studying, they say, 'We know what books you "read" there, and what you "study".'

On the field, we win every game except the final, which we lose to Pakistan. I think their opener, Nasir Jamshed, will play international cricket one day. The Nepal game remains the only one I play, although every day has been a contest, trying to fit myself in what seems like a foreign country where Hindi is the only language and being a student is an insult.

When they ask me at the end of the match when I want to leave, my immediate answer is 'tonight'. I don't even want to wait until the next morning. From Ramanashree Hotel just off the Double Road in Bangalore to back home in Madras is not a long journey, but the two places seem worlds apart to me. On the way back from the ground, I am thinking that I want to get back as soon as possible. That I must pack my bags and leave tonight.

Once I am on *my* way, I tell myself I am not coming back. I no longer want to be here. Where I'm going is *my* well, and I'm one of the best in that well. I'm happy to be there. I am returning to my well. Donning that India blue and batting with Tendulkar is the last thing on my mind. I don't want to feel alienated, belittled, intimidated and humiliated anymore.

Back home in Madras, I am more at peace with myself. I carry my India Under-17 kit to cricket practice. I help St Bede's thrash Santhome in the traditional school cricket rivalry. I notice that I've returned as a better cricketer. The biggest difference is in my fitness level. Earlier, I would hit to mid-off and mid-on and just stand there. Now, I take singles every time. I am dropping and running. Without realizing, I learned all these things in the nets, from Venky speaking about it during idle time and watching others do it during the games.

To score at a run a ball in school cricket is unheard of, but I am scoring 80s in 65 balls and hundreds in 80 balls, and am doing it regularly. I train in my India team gear. I can overhear people talking about how good I have become. They point to my kit. They call me the 'India player' behind my back. Bowlers are tentative bowling to me. I have a presence. Oh god, it means something. I enrol myself in private Hindi classes.

5

Amma plants the offspin bowling seed in my mind, but Anirudha Srikkanth nurtures it. The vibe between us was cold as two of the five roommates at the Sea Green Hotel in Bombay, competing for what we knew was going to be the sole spot from Tamil Nadu in that India Under-17 side. When I return to Madras and start to play age-group cricket for Tamil Nadu, I sense no animosity from Anirudha, who is also the captain of the side. I have none either.

Anirudha is the first captain to seriously use me as a spin bowler in 'days cricket'. Multiple-day matches with no limit on the number of overs a team can bat are called days cricket in India. I have always been the last throw of the dice for other captains.

Anirudha, though, loves me to bits for my bowling. I don't know why. Even when he wasn't the captain, he would keep asking the captain to bring me on to bowl. Perhaps he is just amused, or perhaps he has his father's eye for talent. Amused because I am constantly changing my actions. Sometimes I copy Harbhajan Singh's bowling action, whom I consider a hero after he single-handedly beat Australia in 2000–01, sometimes Ramesh Powar. Sometimes I bowl offspin; on the odd occasion, I bowl legspin with the same action, but I invariably get him wickets. Every time he gives me the ball, I pick up wickets. Before lunch, before tea, before drinks, whenever.

In limited-overs cricket, I have been bowling defensively for a long time. Right from our school days, we've had this strategy of using four offspinners from the 11th over to the 50th. Yo Mahesh and J. Kaushik share our first 10 overs, after which four of us bowl 10 each unchanged. Guru Kedarnath and Santosh are frontline spinners; Vijay Rahul and I are batters who can bowl part-time offspin. Kedar and Vijay go from 11 to 30; Santosh and I bowl from 31 to 50.

We rarely break our spell. Everyone has his own style; everybody bowls economically. My field is usually short third, backward point, point, cover, sweeper, mid-off, long-on, short midwicket and deep square leg. And I bowl wide outside off for the cut. Except I am too quick for most batters. Quick, quick, quick. And then the odd slower, flighted offbreak. I am not yet bowling the *sodakku* in matches.

Santosh is the slower classic offspinner until he lets rip a *doosra*, which zips off the surface. It is the ball when the bowler shows you an offbreak but takes it the other way. It is almost unplayable because it is extremely difficult to pick from the hand. In most cases, it requires bending and straightening the arm, which is illegal. Bowlers at the international level continue to bowl the *doosra*, but Santosh is sent to correct his action. When he comes back with a corrected action, he has lost the *doosra*. And because he is slow in the air, we don't use him for the last 20 overs.

At the Parle G school cricket event, Santosh and I found ourselves defending around 60 runs in the last 20 overs. I told Santosh, 'Let's take it over by over. If you can go at 3 an over, I will make sure I don't concede the other 30 from my end.' I bowled my 10 overs for 16 runs and three wickets, the wickets coming in the last over as the batters hit out looking for the 6 runs that they needed.

Yet, C.K. Vijayakumar, our coach at St Bede's, tells me neither to write 'offspinner' in the forms we fill for age-group selections for Tamil Nadu nor bowl offspin at the trials. I don't. He is a well-respected coach who never wishes ill of anyone, so I say okay and move on. I don't need to save his number in the DigiBook because his is one of the few numbers I remember by heart.

Even when I am passing out of school, he tells me not to classify myself as an offspinner for the selection trials. I agree again. This time, though, he calls me back when I am walking away. He asks me why I am blindly agreeing with him for two years. I tell him I know why he says that to me. He knows I can get in as a batter, so why create extra competition for Santosh and Kedar?

Vijayakumar is pleased with my response, and tells me, 'I can write it and give it to you: you will play for India as an offspinner.'

* * *

Queens Road in Bangalore bustles with breathless activity. The Mahatma Gandhi Park at the junction of MG Road and Queens Road is a designated protest site and usually has crowds around the statue of the Mahatma. The bus stops on either side of the road usually result in traffic jams. Either side of the road is peace: in Cubbon Park and in the M Chinnaswamy Stadium. Traffic cops hide around the corner to trap those jumping the signal. Behind where the policemen lean against their bikes is the boundary wall of the M. Chinnaswamy B Ground, which is used for training by the National Cricket Academy (NCA).

I have been here before with Thatha, when I played for TSR in an Under-14 club tournament as a nine-year-old. With the Tamil Nadu Under-14 and Under-17 teams; with the Madras Under-16 team for the Parle G tournament; and with the India Under-17 team. The space that was used for dormitories and random storage has now become the NCA. This time it is for a month-long Under-19 camp, which will lead the way for selection for the 2006 Under-19 World Cup to be held in Sri Lanka.

The first thing we are told upon reaching the NCA is to be ready for our fitness tests at 10 a.m. the next morning. I have taken class tests, practical tests, theory tests, unit tests and annual tests, but this is a first. This will be a proper assessment of our fitness and strength. The only fitness I know of is running laps of the grounds.

I have no idea what awaits me. In the push-up test, we're made to do continuous push-ups within a certain time frame.

I fail to reach ten. To check our abdominal strength, they ask us to do crunches. I can barely cross twenty. In the sprint test, we are asked to do six laps of the pitch and then repeat it after a thirty-second break.

Ravindra Jadeja and Anirudha ace the tests. Everyone likes them. Especially Jadeja, because he is an exceptional fielder and an excellent bowler. He looks too young and too small to be there. I score four on 100, which is second from the bottom.

Shankar Basu, the man in charge of these tests, seems to have made up his mind that I am a shirker. Every time he sees me, he makes a nasty comment. 'Who are you? Where have you come from? You've never done fitness, is it? Has your body ever seen sweat?' When I've had enough, I go to his office and tell him, 'Listen, sir, I have no knowledge of training. But I will do whatever you say for the next month. You will see my level of commitment then, and you can make a decision.'

Basu gives me a cursory glance and sends me off, saying, 'Okay, we will see. Go now.'

As I am leaving, with my body still getting used to the intense physical work it has just been put through, I tell him, 'Also, sir, I have some pain in my hamstring. Can you look at it while I am here?'

That's it. Basu loses it. 'Who do you think I am? Do you not even know the difference between a physiotherapist and a trainer? Go find the physiotherapist. His name is Muthu.'

It's fair to say we haven't got off on the right foot. To add to that, Basu is also Anirudha's personal trainer, and Anirudha has done really well in the fitness test. However, Ani does have a weakness for ice cream and milkshakes. We get breakfast coupons for Adiga's, a small restaurant in the clubhouse, and lunch and dinner are given to us in the residential wing.

Next to Adiga's is an ice-cream shop, which also sells juices and milkshakes. Ani indulges for the first couple of days, but Basu puts an end to it. Ani is quite used to standing up for us and fighting for things, but now his own indulgence has been brought to an end. Now he has to wait for that one special day when they will give us milkshakes as part of the approved diet.

The day we get milkshakes, they are watery. He asks the catering manager, 'How much did you drink? How much water did you put in this?' Ani gets a rude reply, and he picks up the glass and marches all the way to the NCA, which is at the other end of the complex, and places the glass at the table of Colonel K.R. Nair, the director of the NCA.

'Sir, please check this and tell me what it is.'

Ani's complaint results in a review meeting and a better milkshake. We need to put this on some noticeboard so that future batches know whom to thank for a good milkshake.

* * *

Not for the first time I find myself in a situation where nobody gives me a chance. I suspect nobody wants to give me a chance. My response is the only one I know: work harder, run harder, push harder.

My 'partner' during the fitness work is Cheteshwar Pujara, whom everybody calls Chintu. The role of a partner is to keep track of how many reps of an exercise his partner manages. This is how it normally goes. You are doing push-ups and, after a while, lose count. When you are done, the partner says you've done thirty. 'How many should I write?' he asks you. You tell him the number you want. And the favour is duly returned the other way around.

The first time I am marking Pujara, I tell him he has done twenty-two and ask him how many he would like me to write down. 'Twenty-two,' he says. Then, when I do the push-ups, he doesn't even ask me how many he should write down.

By the end of the camp, my score goes from four to sixty-four. I ace all the running tests. The only thing holding me back is my core strength, which results in ordinary scores in the push-up and abdominal strength tests. Even Basu has taken a liking to me. He is talking about me to everyone. I can feel everyone talking about me. I feel I am not as unfit as others have made me believe I am.

Dilip Vengsarkar, head of the BCCI's Talent Research Development Wing (TRDW), makes an appearance one day.

He takes me aside and operates the batting machine just to watch me bat. He works with me on the grip. In between, I fly to Madras for a day for my interview at an engineering college. Unlike Ani's march to his office, I tentatively approach Colonel Nair for leave for one day. When he finds out it is for my college admission, the NCA pays the airfare too.

Parthasarathi Sharma, the batting coach at the camp, asks for big-turning pitches towards the end, and I excel on them too. They make me the captain of the NCA team in an internal match, and I make 165 runs followed by seven wickets with my off-spin bowling. Then another century and six wickets in the next match.

Towards the end of the camp, Vengsarkar and the coaches signal me to come to them. They are having tea outside Adiga's. They tell me that, for the Under-19 World Cup, they are looking at me as a middle-order batter who also contributes with the ball. They also tell me they are impressed with my leadership qualities. I leave the camp on a real high, already an India Under-19 player-in-waiting in my mind. I am thinking of all the names who have recently played in the Under-19 World Cup for India: Yuvraj Singh, Harbhajan Singh, Dinesh Karthik, Mohammad Kaif and Parthiv Patel.

* * *

I find myself overqualified for the lower-division leagues in Chennai, but I score runs and take wickets ruthlessly. All these runs help me land a contract with Southern Petrochemical Industries Corporation (SPIC) for 2004–05. A.C. Muttiah is the chairman of SPIC. Cricket patronage runs in his blood. He is the son of industrialist M.A. Chidambaram after whom the Chepauk stadium is named.

We have a tough year, failing to win a single game. In one of our last matches, fighting relegation, I score 88 against a strong Indian Overseas Bank (IOB) attack. We still lose, but at least not by an innings. Appa is watching from the stands. After the game, D. Vasu, a former Tamil Nadu all-rounder who has just retired from first-class cricket, approaches Appa.

Vasu, captain of Alwarpet, one of the two league teams owned by Chemplast, likes to watch teams fighting relegation because his team doesn't have the budget to compete for the star players. He likes to pick players from smaller teams. He needs no introduction when he goes over to Appa, who has watched him play at the Teachers College ground and the YSCA ground.

'Sir, I want your son to play for Alwarpet,' Vasu tells Appa. 'We can pay him Rs 7500 per month.'

That is the high end of the regular pay. I get Rs 1000 at SPIC. I am excited. It turns out that Appa is more excited than I am. He springs out of his seat and says, 'Sir, playing under you is enough. We don't need the money.'

When we reach home, it is evening and Amma is restless. 'Where is your phone?' she asks Appa. 'I called and called before I left office.'

Amma had only recently bought us two Sony Ericsson T10 mobile phones. She doesn't have one herself, but she needs to keep tracking us as we wander to cricket and movies. Clearly, in his excitement at seeing Vasu, Appa forgot to pick up his phone from where he was sitting. By the time we get back to SPIC, it is pitch dark. We look in every nook and corner but don't find the phone.

Losing the phone has dampened Appa's excitement a little, but there's no sadness that a call from Chemplast can't fix. Bharath Reddy, the cricket in-charge at Chemplast, who once chided Appa for trying to push his little boy into the Jolly Rovers nets, is now calling on him to send the same son to play for Jolly Rovers as an offspinner.

Appa is glad he hasn't agreed to be paid by Vasu. To him, playing for the Jolly Rovers is bigger than playing for a World XI. He wouldn't have had the tact to pull out of the deal with Vasu had he agreed on money. Now he won't feel guilty for turning Vasu down.

Except that he won't have to. I want to play for Alwarpet, for a captain who saw me play in a relegation match and identified me as a talent. Besides, I am unlikely to get any batting opportunities in a team that has Sujith Somasunder, Vikram Kumar, Hemang

Badani and Dinesh Karthik. I tell Vasu about the offer from the Jolly Rovers, and he raises his offer to Rs 15,000.

Appa is aghast. 'I didn't know you could be so cheap,' he tells me. 'You are selling the game for some money.' I fail to convince him that I have chosen Alwarpet CC over Jolly Rovers for cricketing reasons. Not that it matters what Appa thinks of me because we have another crisis approaching.

R.I. Palani's team, Indian Bank, has managed to work its way into the first division, and he wants me to play for his team. The situation is tricky enough to warrant a family conference. I must choose between a captain who saw me play and valued me in an organic manner, a team full of stars that Appa wants me to play for and a man who has seen me back from my school days and wouldn't take no for an answer.

Appa makes the first choice for me, saying that Indian Bank's team doesn't even have a home ground or proper training facilities. Deciding that, though, is the easier part. Breaking the news to Palani is not easy. So we decide to buy a box of sweets and a basket of fruit and pay a visit—all three of us—to Palani at his residence.

Appa stammers out the message that he is honoured that Palani thought me worthy of playing for him, but unfortunately, I can't. As he speaks, I can sense that he is incredibly tense. Palani calmly asks the loaded question, 'Why?' I immediately repeat my father's reasoning: 'Because Chemplast have better facilities. It will help me as a cricketer.' Even before I can finish the sentence, I feel Appa's disapproving fist holding my hand. He goes, 'Keep quiet, keep quiet. I don't want you to talk about this. Let the grown-ups deal with this.'

Despite not raising his voice, Palani makes sure we know he is extremely upset. He says he has supported me throughout my school career, and playing for his team will only enhance my reputation. It will be a better career choice as Under-19 and Under-22 selections are around the corner.

I respond:, 'Sir, you've been of great help to me. It was only after joining your team that I played in the Under-17 category for India, and it has been one of the brightest moments of my life. But going forward, I think I need to improve as a cricketer for which better facilities will be essential. And I'm sorry, sir, I can't play for your team for that reason. And thank you very much for your support so far.'

Palani still doesn't raise his voice and says, 'This is your decision, and you will have to live with it.' I just thank him again, and we leave.

On the way back, in our second-hand Hyundai Santro, Amma gives me a piece of her mind. She says, 'You shouldn't have been the one doing the talking with Mr Palani. Everybody will feel you talk too much for your age.'

'They already feel that way,' Appa says, who has so far been silent, probably worrying if I have ended up offending an important official. He goes on to say that since I have 'dealt with' the Palani situation myself, I shouldn't need their help dealing with the little situation at Chemplast.

Very well, then, I say, and seek an appointment with Bharath Reddy. I tell him, 'Sir, I'll be extremely delighted to play for Jolly Rovers. I am glad you see my bowling potential, but I want to bat, and Jolly Rovers have so many batters. So this year, I will play for Alwarpet.'

He tells me there is no guarantee that he will ever consider me for the Jolly Rovers again if I play for Alwarpet.

* * *

Already a future India Under-19 player in my mind and a player for whom three first-division teams are competing, I return to the Tamil Nadu Under-19 side for the Vinoo Mankad Trophy and inform them that I want to play in the middle order and bowl a lot more. I am fit, way fitter than my teammates, and I feel my game is at another level right now. There is no resistance to this demand.

We run roughshod over the whole South Zone, even the formidable Karnataka. In two of the matches, I hardly get to bat or bowl because our fast bowlers make excellent use of the conditions, but in others, I make contributions both with the bat and the ball. I take nine wickets at an average of 16 and go at 3 runs per over to go with handy runs whenever I get the chance to bat.

Five days later, I am not part of the South Zone squad despite being one of the most successful players on the most successful side in the zone. Bowlers with fewer wickets make it ahead of me. By now, the nets have begun for Tamil Nadu Under-19 for the days format. I am so dejected at my non-selection that it feels like I am dragging my dead body into these nets. It is in this state that I walk past the Tamil Nadu representative on the South Zone selection committee without greeting him. As I walk past him, he makes it a point to greet me. I don't react and walk to the nets.

The next day, I am summoned by Palani, who is now the director of cricket at TNCA. He has already received the complaint from the selector regarding my 'disrespectful' behaviour. Palani asks me what my problem is. 'Sir, I don't know why you think the problem is with me,' I say. 'They have picked a South Zone team without me when I have done so well.'

And Palani goes, 'How many hundreds did you score?'

I say, 'Sir, it is not easy to score hundreds in the middle order. Besides, this was a low-scoring tournament. I've contributed whenever the team has needed it, and I've also taken nine wickets and finished my quota of overs in every game. Everybody at the NCA rated my bowling along with my batting and wanted me to take on the all-rounder role. This is what they want me to do going forward.'

Palani says, 'The selectors have told me they have not considered you an offspinner here.'

The next day, I get a call from Vivek Jaisimha, Vengsarkar's colleague at TRDW. 'Why is your name not on the South Zone team list?' he asks. 'I saw your reports from the NCA. The coaches had a lot of good things to say about your batting, bowling and leadership. It is disappointing to see you are not a part of the South Zone team. I have even come to know you were not even considered as an offspinner.' Later, Vengsarkar calls me up as well.

I say nothing can be done now, and I disconnect the call. When I sit back and think that a legend of Indian cricket has taken the trouble of finding out my phone number and making this call, it makes me feel even worse about the non-selection. I go and have another conversation with Palani. I tell him of the calls that I have received. I tell him how helpless I feel.

Palani says, 'Whatever is done is done,' and that I should now focus on days cricket.

* * *

When I report to the Alwarpet nets for the 2005–06 season, I discover that even Vasu wants to use my offspin. He wants me to be the batting all-rounder in his side. Not again, I think. I have already burned my fingers once. But as someone who has rejected two other sides, I think I have some leverage here, and I demand the opening slot in the side. 'I will not bat elsewhere.'

I am paired with M. Vijay. It is not easy to figure him out immediately, and we don't have enough time to get to know each other well. Our opening partnership never gets off. When I am washing my face after the fourth failure, Vasu casually asks me if I think opening is working *for me*.

'Yes,' I say. 'Why? What happened?'

Vasu says, 'I think you should focus more on your offspin. I brought you here because you can do both. That is what made you successful at SPIC. Right now, you are focusing too much on your batting, and it's not working out. I gave you four matches. Now I want you to bat in the middle order, and we will give you enough overs. Just try it. It will work.'

So, I bat in the middle order and bowl a lot of overs. It is an education watching Vasu operate. He is a versatile bowler who has taken five-fors in first-class cricket both as a left-arm fast bowler and as a left-arm spinner. Now, though, he just bowls spin. He was a good enough batter to have scored three first-class hundreds. Standing at mid-on or mid-off, I grasp all I can from watching him bowl. There are times when he has taken one wicket out of the top five, but if he gets a sniff to make it two out of six, it is a sight to watch him run through the lower order and take a five-for. How he piles that pressure with on the field placements. How he talks. To the umpire, never to the batter. The batter only gets a stern, cold stare from him.

Vasu says you should never communicate with the batter. If you communicate with them, they feel comfortable. Never let them feel comfortable. If anybody in our team communicates with a batter, Vasu has a go at them. 'As an XI, if you cannot come together against the batter, then it's as good as you taking my money and not being loyal to me.' He likes crowding a batter without saying anything to them.

To play under Vasu is to learn that taking wickets is an art completely different from building your control with repetitions. To quickly find out what a batter is not comfortable with and then use it to build up to a wicket. Sometimes he holds my hand through it. I usually bowl with a left-arm spinner's field: five fielders on the off side, four on leg. I bowl wide outside off, but in a delicate game against PARRY's, Vasu brings out the proper spinner in me.

We've scored 234; the game is in the balance, and I am the seventh bowler. Gowjith Subhash, an up-and-coming big hitter, is held back till the sixth wicket falls. PARRY's need about 60 at this point. As soon as Vasu sees Subhash, he asks me to send the short midwicket back but still bowl the way I do. I bowl wide, and Subhash lofts me over mid-on for a six.

Vasu tells me not to worry and asks me to bowl the same line. This time, Subhash goes back and cuts. Now Vasu pushes the long-on back and says, 'Do one thing, make sure you bowl straighter lines. Don't give him anything for the cut. If you get hit for a six, it's fine.'

So I bowl straighter. Subhash blocks a couple. And Vasu is coming up to me every ball to tell me what to bowl. This time, he comes and says, 'Toss it up, but bowl a topspinner. On the leg stump.'

The top spinner hurries off the surface and doesn't turn sideways. It also tends to bounce more. But the leg stump? 'Just bowl on the leg stump, he won't sweep,' Vasu tells me.

So I do that. On cue, Subhash tries a big hit but not the sweep and gets a top edge to deep midwicket. For eighteen-year-old me, this is magic. This is when I realize I know how to bat and I know how to bowl the ball, but wicket-taking is not about bowling the ball, hitting the pads or getting somebody bowled. It is something else. Vasu goes on to talk me through two more wickets. We end up with an 8-run lead, which gives us 5 points to their 2.

Throughout the rest of the season, I learn how to set my fields from Vasu. I learn a lot of intricate things: when to push the midwicket back, when to keep the mid-on up, when to really put the fielder back and what you do when you put the fielder back. In the final few games, I score a couple of fifties and end the season with 16 wickets, feeling upbeat once again.

The next season, Vijay moves to Jolly Rovers. I want to move too. Or perhaps I am not sure I want to move; I just want to see interest in me. I want to feel wanted. I want to feel like I have grown as a cricketer. I want to see how my performances are being seen at the end of the season. I call someone in their office to test the waters and casually ask them if there are any openings at Jolly Rovers.

'There might be openings, but not for you,' I am told.

I feel spurned again. It is the coconut oil and blackboard situation again. I see someone telling me I can't be good enough for Jolly Rovers. I now have no choice but to show them that I am too good for them.

In the next season, I turn out for Alwarpet, bat in the middle order, and score 727 runs, including four hundreds, the same as the great S. Sharath's long-standing record. And I have 40 wickets to go with it. By the end of the season, Vasu isn't setting fields anymore. I am setting the fields. For myself and others. However, I have missed too many semester exams by now and have to pull out of the knockouts to answer my engineering college exams.

When I am leaving, Vasu tells me: 'Look, I'd love for you to play for Alwarpet, but I don't think it's correct for you, or for me or from a cricketing perspective that you stay with Alwarpet. The bird has grown. It's got wings. You move on to Jolly Rovers now. I can't do anything about it. Neither can you. You have to go there.

'But let me tell you something. I will really miss having a helping hand like yours on the team. If you were 32–33, I would have handed the team over to you. I would have left the team and retired. But you have a strong future. Just make sure you work on your fitness.'

S. Ramesh, the former India opener who stands at slip for me, writes a nice article about me in the *Deccan Chronicle*. Even he asks me to watch my weight.

This is the season I start to believe I can make a career as an offspinner who bats in the middle order. This is the year I get into the Ranji Trophy probables. Nobody tells me I have scored too many runs or taken too many wickets for my age.

6

Arts. Commerce. Science. Science split into engineering and medicine. These are extremely difficult and important decisions that every school kid in India makes around the age of 18. This is not a decision any of the boys at the India Under-17 camp are making. For me, I have no other option. My family has made it clear that I cannot put all my eggs in one basket. If cricket doesn't work out, I have to be able to make a living for myself. For that, I have to go through college education, and I am not allowed to pick the easier streams that other athletes choose in Madras: arts or commerce.

Amma wants me to study medicine. Her sister is a doctor. She has seen the respect doctors command in society. I want to study commerce so that I can focus on my cricket. Appa sits on the fence, and finally I decide to take up engineering. It sounds like my decision, but it really isn't. I have only chosen the lesser of the evils. Then I have to prove I am worthy of it by taking the entrance exam. I clear the test along with most of my friends, and having played cricket helps at the next stage.

The next stage is called counselling. This is where it is decided which college you go to and which stream you pick. If you clear the test with a good score, you can get into the more prestigious of the colleges. My score in math, physics and chemistry is only half-decent, but points are added to your score if you are a sportsperson of some merit. Having played Under-17 cricket for India makes my score good enough to get into Sri Sivasubramaniya Nadar College, or SSN as it is more commonly known as. Of the three streams offered to me, I pick computer engineering. It may be the lesser evil, but it is still evil. I feel like I will die trying to balance studies and cricket. I don't know when the day starts or it ends. It feels like these four years of my life will never end. Santosh falls short by a few marks and settles for another college 2–3 km from SSN. Aravind doesn't make it either.

Every day is a hustle, trying to manage both college and cricket. I have started noticing name plates outside homes in Madras. Everyone adds their educational qualification next to their name. I wonder if this happens in other parts of India too. I also wonder what my nameplate will say, and I see 'Ravichandran Ashwin, Twelfth Standard.' I can't see a way I can survive practice, college, fitness, matches and exams, both written and practical.

I imagine Appa will be happy with 'Ravichandran Ashwin, Jolly Rovers.' Amma will be like, 'Jolly Rovers? You want to put Jolly Rovers on your nameplate? You are twelfth standard.'

The only time I really enjoy college is during the study leave before exams. This is when I get to spend a lot of time with my friends. We play cricket for four to six hours, but we also manage to study together even though we are all at different colleges.

Santosh is decent at math. There are three days until the math exam, and I don't know what to expect. Santosh says, 'Don't worry, *machan*, there will be three sixteen-mark questions in the exam. My college staff has told me. I will teach you how to solve those.'

If it is a question worth sixteen marks, it is going to go over nine or ten pages. Integral calculus, differential calculus, quadratic equations, the works. We start solving it in the morning and get the hang of it by around 5.30 p.m. This is when we give each other high fives and get ready to get some fresh air, coffee and snacks only to realize Aravind has been texting a girl and asks us, 'What next?'

Santosh repeats the process for Aravind, and we go out for our break. When we return, we ask Aravind if he has the answer.

Without looking away from the phone, he says, 'Yes'. 'What is the answer?' '1D,' he says. We look at each other, wondering how he has come up with a bus route.

We take a peep in to his notebook and find out that he has cancelled X and X of DX as if it is a simple arithmetic fractions equation instead of the complicated integral and differential calculus, which it is. Differentiation and integration are the most basic part of engineering. Without knowing them, you can't get far. We know then and there that Aravind is going to spend all his engineering in arrears when it comes to math exams. We nickname him XDX Aravind.

Another friend of ours who is going to have huge arrears by the end of the semester is Raju. He never studies; just plays cricket, and not very well. But he wants to play for India, which he professed with a broken pickle bottle on his bicep on a hot day years ago. He wants to make Tamil films too.

Raju's mother asks us to help him out with his studies. I have done well in a paper called 'Electronic devices and circuits'. So I take it upon myself to guide him through that. Like Santosh earlier, I know which sixteen-mark questions are certain to be in the exam. I tell Raju all about RC oscillators and LC oscillators, one of which will definitely be in the paper. 'This is how you make the switch.' I teach him everything I know.

The next day, we are all sitting in Raju's room—Raju, his brother Bhuvnesh, my cousins Vicky and Shyam, two of Raju's school friends and myself. I ask him for the question paper, and I get really excited seeing the RC oscillator question in his exam. There, that's sixteen marks, I think. I ask Raju how he answered it. Silence. I ask again, 'I showed you the LC oscillator and then the slight change for the RC oscillator. Did you get it right?' Silence. Then I ask again. Again silence.

Just as Raju is about to open his mouth, Aravind Srinivas, one of his friends, starts singing, '*Muthumani rathinangalum.*' The song is an S.P. Balasubrahmanyam classic that he sang in one breath, but it is used as a comedy prop in the movie *Pasupathi c/o Rasakkapalayam.* Comedian Vivek, playing a goofy cop, breaks into this song every time a person he is interrogating doesn't have an answer for him.

The whole room bursts out laughing. And then his other friend asks me, 'Anna, have you seen his answer sheets from the last semester? He wrote movie scripts there.'

I find it strange that he knows what Raju wrote in his exam papers.

His friend says, 'After he failed the exam, he returned home and said he answered the paper well, but he failed because a mistake must have been made in the evaluation. So, he put Rs 1400 for a re-evaluation, and got his answer sheet. It had stories for his future movie projects.'

As we all laugh, Raju has drifted away to speak to his girlfriend on the phone. There is a temple procession outside the window. Raju asks his girlfriend to place the earpiece on her forehead. While he convinces her to do so, he also finds some kumkum, a red turmeric powder. Among other things, it is applied to the forehead of married women.

'Is the phone next to your forehead?'

'Yes.'

'There is a temple procession going outside. We have a tradition that during this procession, husbands apply kumkum to the forehead of their wives. I just applied it to my phone. I hope you received it.'

Not sure if she has received something, but we have got our share of laughs during intense exams.

* * *

Madrasi.

Of, or from, Madras.

Technically, it should mean not more than the Hindi word for someone or something from Madras. Like Punjabi from Punjab or Gujarati from Gujarat. I make an exception here for Madras not being a state, let alone all of southern India. I also don't go into the semantics of the name change from Madras to Chennai.

But I can't understand why players from the rest of India expect me to feel embarrassed or small when they disparagingly say, '*Yeh toh* Madrasi *hai*.' Oh, he is a Madrasi.

I am from Madras, and I am proud of it even though it is now called Chennai. I will forever be proud of the city on whose streets I've spent most of my life. Playing cricket, talking cricket, celebrating festivals and New Year's, building friendships, travelling these streets to go to cricket practice and the movies, the buses on these streets.

I am proud of the language we speak. *Madrasi* to others, Tamil is a delightful language befitting the colourful, full-of-life city that Chennai is. I speak a language that is native to us. I find it awkward to have to explain to people that this language is the oldest spoken and living language in India, possibly the whole world. What's wrong with our language?

One thing that bothers me about Chennai, though, is that we love to talk a good game. All the Uncles in the stands can spend entire afternoons talking about the joys of watching cricket. Whenever they see a young spinner, they speak in essays about Venkat and Prasanna. Or Laker and Lock if they are trying extra hard. Or of the times when there was a young Tamil Nadu batter who batted like Viv Richards but was never given the opportunity.

It seems to me that we romanticize the game more and play it less. Which is why we haven't had steady representation in the national team since Kris Srikkanth. We haven't even won a Ranji title since 1987–88. I, though, have seen the future of Tamil Nadu cricket and Indian cricket. His name is Dinesh Karthik. He is unlike any player I have seen in Chennai.

I watch a lot of cricket matches. Sometimes with Appa and sometimes alone. I've heard a lot about T. Kumaran's pace, and he does let it fly on matting pitches, but he doesn't make it to the next level. I have seen S. Ramesh, S. Sharath and Hemang Badani, but Karthik is something else.

Karthik is a little over a year older than me. We've both played a lot of school cricket, and he has dominated every team. He is the only one to have played for five different schools. He changes schools every year because he falls short on attendance, but he is such a good cricketer that there is a demand for him to join new schools. It is unheard of in Chennai. He is my hero for being able to do that.

At seventeen, Karthik is representing Tamil Nadu in Under-19 cricket. I make sure to cycle to the grounds he is playing at. He scores double hundreds in two sessions. It's the closest thing to watching Virender Sehwag bat live. Bowlers are scared of bowling to him. He sweeps, slog-sweeps and steps out. It is fun to watch him bat against spin.

In the Under-19 World Cup of 2004, India's captain Ambati Rayudu is banned for a match for time-wasting against Sri Lanka. Karthik is then made captain, which is a moment of personal pride for me.

Nobody wears sunglasses in Tamil Nadu cricket, but Karthik has returned with a big case of sunglasses. I watch from a distance to try and learn whatever I can because I know he is going to be an India player. Even the way he pads up is different: he puts one pad on, taps it twice and then straps it on. Then he does the same with the other pad.

At the Ranji Trophy semi-final against the Railways in 2003–04, the Chennai Uncles are talking up Kulamani Parida in the stands at Chepauk Stadium. They are not parochial, as we have seen during the Test against Pakistan, but they can take the romanticizing too far. During the first two days, all I hear is how much Parida is turning the ball and how nobody is picking him. Tamil Nadu have lost two quick wickets towards the end of the day, and in comes my hero at No. 8.

Parida is bowling the last over of the day. Karthik has just walked in, and he steps out and hits Parida for a six. I am like, 'Wow, who does these things?' My whole idea of watching cricket for almost two years becomes watching Karthik. I am so fascinated that I even drag Appa with me wherever Karthik is playing.

Months later, Karthik is playing for India as a schoolboy cricketer. Steve Harmison gets him out for 1, and I am heartbroken. This is one cricketer who I think will play for India and pave the way for other Tamil Nadu cricketers, but he is out for 1. When will he play next? In the second innings, though, Karthik collects a wide miles down the leg side and acrobatically stumps Michael Vaughan, looking like a ballet dancer in that moment. I find my excitement back. India go on to win. For days after this, I make sure to watch the highlights just to relive this moment over and over again.

* * *

I start expecting a Ranji Trophy call-up in the winter of 2006. I've fully transitioned into an offspinner who can bat. After Vasu's mentoring at Jolly Rovers, I find a sounding board in Sunil Subramaniam, the left-arm spinner who played for Tamil Nadu in the 1990s. The one thing he instils in me is to spin the ball hard. And that's what I begin to be known for: the revolutions I put on the ball, which in turn, result in movement in the air and then off the pitch. He also wants me to bowl the 'attacking line' outside off.

I read in the newspapers that Aashish Kapoor, Tamil Nadu's offspinner then, is getting on, and there is a need to get in a youngster. On top of that, V.B. Chandrasekar, the selector, names me in the probables in the pre-season in 2006–07. I am in the camp where I meet W.V. Raman, the former India batter and now the coach of Tamil Nadu. He shows an interest in what I am doing after having followed my progress in club cricket. He tells me how accuracy is most important for a spinner and how looking for wickets is not.

I am certain I will make the final fifteen, but I don't. Aashish Kapoor does. I hear people talk about how Raman and Aashish are good friends because they've played a lot of cricket together. I don't know either of them personally, but I have formed an opinion subconsciously, even though Raman has paid a lot of attention to me in the pre-season camp. Not being selected can do this to you.

So the team goes to Delhi for the season opener without me. M. Vijay, Virat Kohli and Ishant Sharma make their first-class debuts in this match. I closely follow the updates on Cricinfo because I am just raring to go. I feel I can make a difference because I am in amazing form. We win the toss but go on to concede the first-innings lead. Aashish bowls 27 overs for no wicket.

In the second match against Andhra in Madras, we take a huge first-innings lead but fail to close out for an outright win. Outright wins in home games are crucial: they get 4 points as opposed to just the 2 for a first-innings lead. We have made a turning track just to blast away Andhra, but we can't. Aashish again gets just the two wickets in 40 overs. The pressure is building, and I am finally called up for the next match against Haryana.

A distant cousin of mine, who is V.B. Chandrasekar's friend, calls me after the game to convey the message from VB: that I have been selected. I have to go to the TNCA office before the match to collect the letter congratulating me for being selected for the Tamil Nadu Ranji side and to collect my whites, the size for which they have from the probables camp. We have one net session before the match, and I can hardly get sleep before my debut. I reach Chepauk pretty early in my second-hand blue Santro car, only to find someone else there before me.

We have a makeshift dressing room for this match. I see a laptop on a bench and a man with a camera in his hand and a tripod next to him. He looks busy, working with cables and walking up and down with equipment. Going by his purposeful air and the equipment around him, I assume he must be an important person. I say, 'Anna, good morning.'

'Yeah, yeah, good morning.'

I mix up my questions: 'Anna, where should . . . when will?'

'Hey, don't disturb me,' he says dismissively.

After some time, I ask him, 'What are you doing?'

He then tells me, 'I am the analyst of your team, Laxmi Narayanan. I am setting up the camera.'

This is the first time I have known of our team filming the game, even though it is just one camera.

The team is more familiar and welcoming than the analyst. I know S. Badrinath, the captain, from Chemplast. Anirudha

Srikkanth is my friend. M. Vijay has been my opening partner. I have given throwdowns to S. Sharath. It doesn't feel like I'm in a new dressing room.

Sharath, the most capped Tamil Nadu player, presents me with my cap. He says, 'I've seen you bowl. I played against you. I think you're all but destined. You know, I think you've got the ability to make 2000 runs and get 200 to 250 first-class wickets. You're that sort of a cricketer. We expect that from you for Tamil Nadu.'

We lose the toss and are asked to field. I take the first wicket to fall. Even though it takes us 27 overs to get the first wicket, we have conceded just 52 runs. Sumeet Sharma, one of the openers, tries to break the shackles by charging at me, but gets beaten in the flight and is bowled. My first first-class wicket. I end the first day with two wickets and go on to get two more.

When I come back into the dressing room, Raman says, 'Well done. That's a lot of work, young man. How do you feel?'

And I say, 'Yeah, sir. I've done that for Alwarpet. So yeah.'

'Forty-eight overs?' he asks.

'Yes, sir,' I tell him. 'I have bowled 30 overs in a day consistently, and after 30 overs, I have also gone to the nets and bowled. So I think I'm ready for this. I'm prepared for this sort of hard work.'

I go into bat at 117 for 7 and get duck-out. The ball that gets me out, I feel I don't have time to face the offspinner, Gaurav Vashisht. Even though we concede the first-innings lead, I take two more in the second. I don't quite ask him in front of all the seniors, but on the third evening I go to Laxmi and say, 'What will the laptop show now?'

'Full video,' he says.

Immediately, I want to watch myself bowl and see how I look when I do so. So I tell him that I want to see my bowling. He shows me a couple of balls before shooing me away. 'I'm busy. Come back later.'

We can't bowl out Haryana to give ourselves a chance on the final day. At the team meeting after this disappointment, I tell the team leaders that they should send me as a nightwatchman if there is an opportunity. My score in the match, which has given me the confidence to say all this to the seniors: duck-out. Raman's feedback to me is to maintain control and accuracy. After the team meetings are over, I ask Laxmi again, 'Anna, can you show me the footage? I want to see myself bowl.'

Laxmi dismisses me again: 'We've just lost. I am very busy for the next two days. Come back after that.'

The next day, I return with a Moser Baer CD and a case for it. Post the nets session, I take the CD to Laxmi and request that he burn my bowling portions onto that CD.

'I told you I would be busy for two days, no?' Laxmi says. 'Come after two days, we will talk.'

I tell him, 'Anna, you keep the CD. You can burn it whenever you get the time.'

Two days later, we are about to leave for Rajkot for our next game. I remind Laxmi about the CD, and he cuts me off again, saying, 'Hey, we lost the last game. I have to do a lot of work. You know how busy it is. I have to take all the footage. Go, I will give it to you when I am free.'

I am left out for the match in Rajkot, where I am looking forward to bowling to my training partner, the insatiable batter, Cheteshwar Pujara. However, I am told there is only room for one spinner and that the spinner needs to be a left-arm spinner. C. Suresh plays ahead of me.

We score 500, and when we bowl, we, the extras, sit near the fence should any of the first XI need anything. I am wondering if my boastful exchange earlier has cost me this game. To add to it, people around me start telling me the coach's likes and dislikes. I also wonder if someone else in the leadership doesn't like me.

All these thoughts dissipate when Raman comes and sits next to me. Suresh is bowling, and Raman asks me if I would have done well on this pitch. I say yes without giving any thought to the question.

'Why do you think you'll bowl well on this pitch?' he asks.

I tell him I will look to stifle the runs so that the fast bowlers can exert pressure. He asks me what fields I would take. I tell him the fields and the plans, and I generally feel better now that I am involved. I also realize, looking at the precious little help for Suresh, that it didn't make any cricketing sense to play both of us.

We take the lead against Saurashtra. On the way back, I remind Laxmi about the CD on the flight again. This time, he doesn't snap back. Perhaps because we have done well. Two days later, before the start of the next practice session, he finally gives me the CD. I am so excited at the thought of watching myself bowl that even though I bowl and bat in the nets, all I can think of is finishing the day, going back home and watching that CD. Not a single minute of that nets session registers in my mind.

I take the CD, throw my kitbag in the car, drive fast, get home, put the CD into my hard drive and start watching. The first thing I notice about myself is that I am overweight. However, once I start bowling, I really admire the drift I get. The batter defends. The sixth ball I bowl, I get him out.

Then comes Sunny Singh; I get a nice drift, and he has to defend. The next ball again drifts, and he defends. Again, a forward-defensive. I am wondering which match Raman watched to give me that feedback about accuracy because the video evidence shows me bowling with such superb control. I am going to take this footage to Raman and confront him about the feedback. I am thinking of Aashish Kapoor and his friendship with Raman.

For the next ball, I make Sunny defend again, and R. Prasanna moves in to field and throws the ball to me. Sunny defends again, and Prasanna fields again. Then again, and again. It is only after 7–8 balls of watching Sunny defend and Prasanna field that I realize Laxmi has put this ball on loop after six balls of the previous over.

I don't even know how to react to this. It is only in the next nets session that I see Anirudha and others pulling Laxmi's leg, so I tell them this story to give them more material. Laxmi is apologetic and burns me another CD, this time properly, and becomes my friend.

The next match is at home, against Uttar Pradesh. We score 325 and are about to go out to bowl on the second morning when Raman asks us, 'So what's the plan for this innings?'

'I will try and get five wickets, sir,' I jump in with the reply.

He says, 'First you need to restrict them. You need to bowl tight at one end, wickets will come. When I ask you about plans, you need not talk about wickets.'

'Sir, I only think that I have to get five wickets. I don't know any other way of thinking,' I say.

'Wickets are the end result,' Raman says. 'If you think about that, you will hurt the team.'

I say, 'Sir, I might be saying I want to pick up five wickets, but I know the plans for it.'

Raman tells me, 'You are bowling against Mohammad Kaif and Suresh Raina. They are India players, not club batters.'

I say, 'Let it be, sir, but it doesn't change anything for me. I will make sure I play it like yet another match for Alwarpet or Jolly Rovers, and I will pick up five wickets.'

I go one step further and take six wickets, but Raman is right: Kaif and Raina are not club batters. Raina scores 124, Kaif 88, and UP take a vital 95-run lead. That is a big setback on a home track. We need to get as many runs as we can in the second innings to give ourselves a shot at winning outright. However, we can't score quickly enough to feel safe with a declaration.

In the end, we get bowled out for 223, setting them 129 in 25 overs for 4 full points. Kaif and Raina make a statement by opening the innings. Now we have to fight for a draw. They both score quickly, and UP reach 66 for 1 in 11 overs. Fast bowlers are going for runs, and the pitch is still good.

I go to S. Badrinath, our captain, and tell him it's time to bowl the way I used to bowl from overs 31 to 50 in club matches. Whatever rough is there for right-hand batters, it is wide. For left-hand batters, there is no rough to play with. And the UP side is full of left-hand batters.

Badri says, 'That is very defensive. Anyway, what field will you have?'

I ask for a slip and no other catchers because the pitch is not doing much. Then a wide gully, a backward point and a cover point. I ask Badri to field at cover. Then I ask for a deep cover, long-off, mid-on and deep square leg.

Badri is perplexed. 'Where will you get your wickets? We can't defend now; we have to take wickets.'

I start bowling wide outside off, and the batters try to go over the leg side. Somebody gets a leading edge to gully, somebody to point, and I fire one in for an lbw, and before you know it, they are 89 for 7, and now it is us pushing for the win and them hanging in for the draw.

UP manage to walk away with the draw, but I have 11 wickets from the match. When I return, I see Raman sitting next to Laxmi, and he immediately gets up to say, 'Well done, young man, you really do know how to pick up wickets.'

I end the Ranji Trophy with 31 wickets at just 16.93 per wicket. We end the tournament on a good note with a thrilling 2-wicket win against Baroda. I take 11 wickets in the match and score the winning runs. For the team, though, it is a disappointing season. We finish seventh in the group of eight.

* * *

Two weeks later, India play against West Indies in an ODI (one-day international) match at Chepauk as part of preparations for the World Cup later in the year. I am asked to bowl at the nets for both teams. International teams invite local bowlers to bowl in the nets because they don't want to exhaust their own bowlers before the actual match. This is my first such invitation.

I am excited at the prospect of bowling to Chris Gayle, Brian Lara, my hero Sachin Tendulkar and the hottest name in Indian cricket today, M.S. Dhoni. I have read about how Imran Khan plucked Waqar Younis out of a nets session even before he had started playing proper domestic cricket. Appa has told me how Kris Srikkanth impressed Sunil Gavaskar in a local game, and that's how he ended up playing for India. These thoughts are not entirely out of my mind. I am going to be bowling in flesh and blood to players I have dreamed of playing with and against.

The West Indies team is the first to arrive for training. Chepauk doesn't have separate nets, so the nets are arranged on the side pitches at the main ground. I bowl to Gayle first. I get him out caught and bowled. Later, I have him edging. I look at him for a reaction because in nets, be it at club level, Ranji Trophy level or anywhere else, the batter nods at you, appreciates you or just says 'bowled', just to acknowledge you. Gayle just picks the ball up and throws it back at me. No eye contact. No reaction.

He gets out, no reaction. He tonks me, no reaction. I think Gayle is probably peculiar, but as I bowl to other batters, it is the same. They smack you, no reaction. They struggle against you, no reaction. Just pick up the ball and bowl again. I find it weird.

And it is not limited to the West Indies players either. India batters are the same. During the India nets, a friend comes and watches from the stands. He wants a photo with Dhoni after the nets so that he can impress girls in college. I, too, am crazy about Dhoni. The way he hits, the way he finishes games, the long hair. He is just a phenomenon.

After we are done, I click a photo with Dhoni myself. I tell him about my friend, and he obliges. My friend is over the moon, but I tell him I am not coming as a nets bowler again. He is stunned. Not only does he want to come and take more photos tomorrow to impress girls, he is generally shocked at me giving up a chance to bowl at these guys.

I tell him what happened. I feel heartbroken. I don't exactly know what I expected when I came to the nets. Yes, those fairy tales of selections of net bowlers are a thought in my mind, but not an expectation. It is something else that has hurt me. I tell my friend I have never been to a cricket match or practice session where nobody has acknowledged me. People try to find out which club you play for or which school or college you study at, but here nobody even asked me what my name was.

I call up the nets organizer who had offered me the gig and tell him I will not be coming tomorrow. Instead, I go to Chemplast and train on my own. I think playing street cricket is more fun than bowling at these internationals. Over the next few days, though, I realize they didn't do it to me because they are bad people. It is just that these are professional cricketers in their bubble, striving for excellence. They must be facing hundreds of bowlers like me. They can't be acknowledging everyone's presence. Worship your heroes from a distance; when you get close to them, be good enough to be one of them.

I don't think any less of my cricket heroes because they didn't acknowledge me when I bowled, but I also don't want to be servicing them with nothing in it for me. I still feel like an ordinary person for servicing them without any acknowledgement when I do well or generally of my effort. So, I don't regret pulling out of the nets. Nor do I want to be just a nets bowler ever again.

7

M.J. Gopalan was Tamil Nadu's pride. He represented India in both cricket and hockey. There used to be an annual match in his honour between Madras and Ceylon. It stopped in 1982, came back for a couple of years in the early 2000s, and then stopped again. After my first first-class season, though, the fixture makes a comeback: Tamil Nadu vs Sri Lanka Cricket XI for the MJ Gopalan Trophy in September 2007, my first travel outside India.

The match is taken so seriously that we are even given a warm-up game before the actual match. And we need all the practice we can get because we are facing a tough side. Almost all the players in the Sri Lanka Cricket XI are knocking at the door of international selection. On the final day of the warm-up match, the Sri Lankan coach comes to me at 3 p.m. and tells me we can call the game off early 'because the final is about to start'.

All of us return to our rooms and get ready to watch the final of the first T20 World Cup between India and Pakistan in South Africa. It is a genuine surprise to everyone that India have made it to the final. The reaction to the new format in India was one of scepticism. The senior players don't even go. Around us, we can hear people talking about this evil format that is going to sully the great old game.

We have only just begun playing the format in India. In fact, Tamil Nadu won the inaugural inter-state T20 tournament under the captaincy of Dinesh Karthik, beating Punjab in the final at Brabourne Stadium. In many matches, I opened the bowling, bringing in all the skills learned in gully cricket and tennis-ball cricket to complement my cricket-ball skills. However, there was little interest in the tournament. It was played in the heat of April, when cricket is rarely played in India.

We begin hearing murmurs of a new T20 league that is signing up players for big money. It is the Indian Cricket League, a rebel tournament that's not sanctioned by the BCCI. Nobody approaches me, but our biggest hitter in the T20 tournament, V. Devendran, joins this tournament along with G. Vignesh.

I have always had an interest in the format because the T20 World Cup introduced me to fantasy cricket. Kris Srikkanth, Anirudha's father, has a cricket website with a new game called 'Captain of Captains', which has been launched with this T20 World Cup. So, I'm closely following the tournament to be able to compete properly on krishcricket.com.

Since Karthik is with the Indian team in South Africa, I am the captain for this M.J. Gopalan Trophy. It has been an amazing ride to watch the Indian team do so well throughout the tournament. The final win leaves us ecstatic.

Two days later, at the Colts Cricket Club Ground in Colombo, we get bowled out for 74. On a damp pitch, we lose the toss and are rolled over by the tall, left-arm quick Chanaka Welegedara and Dhammika Prasad, who is really quick and has already played for Sri Lanka.

I bat well in the second innings but fall lbw to an extraordinary ball from the left-arm spinner Rangana Herath. It speeds off the surface, and instead of turning away, it comes back into me. I am beaten comprehensively, but I think I have noticed something here. Is it? Could it be? Have I seen the *sodakku* with a cricket ball bowled by someone other than the Sri Lankan spinner I saw at the camp in Chennai?

It is indeed the *sodakku*. Even as I walk back, I recall seeing a different grip with a finger sticking out, but I never thought someone as classic as Herath would bowl this out of nowhere.

This is deadlier than what I witnessed at the V.V. Kumar camp because Herath is a perfectly good orthodox spinner and also has this variation.

I return to India intent on working on my own *sodakku*. My suspicion has always been that it would be extremely difficult to bowl with a cricket ball. A tennis ball is different; it is soft and can almost be squeezed between your fingers. But if they are doing it in Sri Lanka, I must work on it too.

* * *

At the camp before the 2007–08 season for Tamil Nadu, Raman comes to me and asks me how I am doing. After the pleasantries are out of the way, he says, 'I want to tell you something. I think you had an amazing run last season. You had your ups and downs, but this year will decide whether you will be only a first-class cricketer or if you have the material and steel to, you know, go on to play for the country. This season will decide that. And normally I don't tell this to people, but I think you will be able to handle yourself. So, I think you should know this.'

It feels flattering and nice. I use the opportunity to tell him about the *sodakku*, how I saw Herath bowl it, how I used to bowl it with the tennis ball, and how I have been working on it with the cricket ball too. He tells me if I could do it with the tennis ball, I should definitely try it with the cricket ball.

I start bowling it in the nets, and it keeps falling short. M. Vijay keeps getting annoyed and starts hitting it with one hand. His reaction suggests I am wasting his time and not servicing him. Badri doesn't show the same disdain, but it is apparent he is not happy either.

It eventually becomes another conversation with Raman. I tell him what I honestly feel. Bowlers are used as blue-collar workers by batters as they wish. Why is it that a bowler apologizes to a batter in the nets if he bowls a bad ball and not the batter if he plays a bad shot? When batters want to practise their big hitting, they slog every ball, no matter what the bowler is bowling. On those days, the bowler can't say it is annoying because he isn't getting the practice he wants. It's the same lab for everyone. If the batter is allowed to play weird shots all day, the bowler should also be allowed to work on different things. I can actually practise without a batter, but the batter needs me. So, he owes it to me not to be annoyed when I am trying something new. I don't want to annoy you, but I want to get better. It's not like I'm only here to make you better.

Raman takes a moment to think and says, 'I think you're right, but since you want to do this seriously, I suggest you go to a net separately and try and do it.'

I am not happy with that solution. 'Sir, he is batting,' I say. 'I'm also plying my trade. He's looking to get better. So am I. If he doesn't want to practise with me, I think he needs to find another net.'

Raman stays calm and says, 'Yeah, you're probably right. But I think we should have this conversation some other time. Right now, we are at a team nets session. Let's not hold it up. We have just two nets and two quality pitches for us to practise. So, if you really want to do this, I can spare you the other pitch.'

As ever, the practical man. If it is a team practice, it is not fair for me to hold it up. He tells me I am not wrong, but he also tells me we need a workable solution. And so, I bowl in a separate net at one stump and do so every day for half an hour before the others arrive.

My relationship with Raman keeps blossoming with almost every nets session. Some might find it annoying, but Raman drills it into me that to play first-class cricket, I must be ruthless and disciplined. I have also realized that I can't just spin the ball hard and expect wickets because these batters can wait for the bad ball. It doesn't always have to be a bad ball either; they can score off good balls too. Raman keeps telling me his favourite phrase: 'Be there and thereabouts all through the day.'

Raman loves challenging people. He teaches me how angular run-ups and alignments work. Then he teaches me about run-up speed and rhythm. What happens if your run-up speed is slower? What if your run-up speed is quicker? What about your stride

Appa, not yet confident of letting me sit behind him on the bike.
This way his arms protect me from falling.

Not the size of the dog in the fight: me with two elder cousins,
Manu and Sriram.

Stylin' and profilin': Looking quite fashionable in the black shirt and white pants on my ninth birthday.

At Amma's office getaway, with Adarsh, her office-best-friend's son.

With Sanjeev and Rajkumar, teammates at PSBB school team.

My first-ever floodlit match. A school's final against Don Bosco at Don Bosco, in kits provided by them.

When tennis-ball cricketers
start playing with the hard ball:
Shyam, getting ready to bat on
the concrete pitch in the home net
erected by Appa.

Heavenly foothills: In
Dharamshala with the
Tamil Nadu Under-19
team; the modern stadium
was still being built.

With the Tamil Nadu Under-19 team. Ani sitting first from right,
Yo Mahesh to my right.

Up for a fight: A Tamil news piece quoted me saying age
fraud is no big deal because eighteen-year-old
kids play thirty-year-old men in international cricket anyway.

Too cool to look directly at the camera: (second from right,
sitting), At an Under-14 Madras vs Tamil Nadu match in
Tirunelveli.

Pre-pre-party: With RUCA boys at Venkat's bachelor party. Planning the rest of the night in a huddle as if going out to the field.

A day out with RUCA boys at a farmhouse on the East Coast Road.

When life gives you lemons: with Prithi and friends.

The two loves of my life: Prithi and RUCA.
(From right) Subash, Bhuvanesh, Sai, Vicky.

Sai to my left, Vivek and Subash to the right.

These paps: Prithi covering her face from
prying eyes.

At a get-together in Nungambakkam.

length and width between the two spinning fingers? And he does it in a practical manner.

First of all, Raman straightens my angular run-up. I get a good drift with my angular run, but Raman teaches me about alignment. In the last season, he told me it was not possible to select me because I was getting both cover-driven and cut. I protested, citing the wickets I had picked. He said he doesn't care about wickets; he wants control.

Now Raman gets down to helping me establish control. He explains that a spinner needs three things: length, line and revolutions on the ball. Revs, he says, can't be controlled; they are almost involuntary. However, if a bowler can control the line by running in a straight line, the length becomes optional. If you are controlling the line, he says, you can vary the length more; the margin of error is greater. I have always heard that for a spinner, 'line is optional, length is mandatory'. It all sounds like rubbish now.

Raman and I are made for each other. For the life of me, I can't keep repeating the same thing. And Raman the coach comes up with something every day to help me keep discovering spin bowling to its fullest. One fine day, he tells me, run in 5 per cent slower today. Then another day, run in 10 per cent faster. Now don't try to spin a mile. Hold it less firmly. He doesn't tell you everything; he just wants you to try it and see for yourself what it does. I do it immediately. And as I do it, I understand the cause and effect. And because it is so instant and practical, I love working with Raman. He makes me realize there is so much more to being a spinner than just imparting the maximum number of revolutions on the ball.

I gradually learn various tricks: width of the crease, slower run-up and different releases. It's all about practical hacks on the go, but for that, you need to try new things and understand the basic cause and effect in the nets. The challenge is to do it without losing revolutions and also staying, as Raman likes to say, there or thereabouts. He doesn't bother much with my field placements.

Badri, the captain, has to. Especially when I am now starting to bring my ideas into how I want to bowl. When I played club cricket, one thing I realized was that the batters were sometimes so good they could hit me over the top of mid-on without even stepping out. However, if I put the man back, in theory giving them an easy single, I used to get them caught at backward short leg or short midwicket. I realized then that even these good batters are not comfortable driving me down the ground, so they go over the top. I realized that they felt the margin of error was greater for them if they went over the top with the field up. So I blocked that option.

In one game, I ask for the mid-on back, and Badri says no. And in the middle of the game, I ask him why. He is the kind of captain who gives his spinners a lot of confidence with his fields. If they get hit over the top, he stays brave and tells them it's okay, that was a good shot. There is no need to set the field back. Now, all of a sudden, he has a spinner who wants the mid-on back even before he has bowled. On top of that, he is asking why he can't get it.

When he realizes I am not going to agree to his field without a proper reason, he says, 'It's too easy to get a single.'

I ask him what if I don't concede a single there.

'Okay then, what is your field?' Badri asks.

I want a long-on back, one short midwicket, one normal midwicket, one backward short leg, one forward short leg and no cover.

'And if you get cover-driven?'

'That's my job,' I say. 'If I get cover-driven, you can take me out of the attack. Or I will bowl to your fields.'

Luckily for me, it works instantly. You can only try to do what you feel is the right thing, but you also need some luck for it to work out. It does, and Badri starts trusting me with my way of bowling. Somehow things tend to work when I team up with Badri. Even last season, when we beat Baroda in a close match, Yusuf Pathan's counterattack threatened to derail us. S. Vidyut was bowling, and I went up to Badri and asked him to put everybody back on the fence except the slip. Badri did, and we immediately got Yusuf out. I am lucky to have a captain who doesn't take offence at my unsolicited advice.

I start the season with six wickets on a Chepauk featherbed and then follow it up with an unbeaten half-century to keep us from losing first-innings points against Maharashtra. Not a bad start to the dreaded second season that everybody speaks about. Bring it on, I say.

Just before the third match, during fielding practice, I go back for a high catch and land on my left wrist. I have had all kinds of injuries in my life, but never a fracture. I have never felt such excruciating pain, and I just know something is wrong. My wrist immediately swells up, and I can't even lift my hand. The scans reveal it has broken in three to four places. In November, right at the peak of the first-class season. Bring on the second season, indeed.

* * *

It has been such a quick turnaround. From being a batter who bowled some seam-up, I am now an offspinner with one-and-a-half successful first-class seasons behind me. I've been playing cricket nonstop, but now with the injury, I have some time to reflect on what my stock trade is.

An offbreak is a delivery that pitches and turns from off to leg for a right-hand batter. Offspin is an art built on offbreaks, but one that needs variations of speed, trajectory and turn to create deception.

To me, offspin bowling—or spin bowling for that matter—is about spinning the ball as hard as I can. Grip it deep in my fingers, impart revolutions on it, and have the right fields for what you are trying to do.

The first bit of deception is created in the air. When I impart so many revolutions to the ball, it drifts away from the right-hand batter, drops late, and lands before they expect it to. That creates a gap between their eyeline and their bat, creating an inside edge, which hits the pad and lobs off for a bat-pad catch, my most common dismissal. My height gives me extra bounce, and I tend to get catches at backward short leg and not forward short leg.

However, batters in first-division club cricket are too good to fall for a single trick. I must induce the other edge too. I get a lot of wickets off the outside edge, but to induce that, I need to keep the inside edge in play. The batter must be bothered by the inside edge, which my big offbreak does.

Still, against good batters, it is not as straightforward as bowling an arm ball and taking the outside edge. Even before bowling the ball that doesn't turn, I must make sure the batter continuously keeps moving back and forward. I can't let the batter be comfortable defending me either off the back foot or the front foot. That means mixing speed, trajectory and angle—whatever it takes. You must throw it up in the air and get a late dip on it. You need to bowl flatter but still go full. I've quickly accumulated all these tricks.

Only then comes into play the art of bowling the delivery that doesn't turn. In longer formats, it can be more lethal than the wrist spinners' wrong'un because the wrong'un can be picked from the hand. When we bowl the one that goes the other way, we do so with an almost identical release.

It is easy to bowl the arm ball or the quicker ball, and it can be picked by the batter through the trajectory or the release. In order to still pitch it up and still keep the trajectory the same, to make it look like an offbreak, and still make it go straight on, I start holding the ball deep in the palm, especially the part close to the base of the thumb, and spin it hard like an offbreak. Because the ball is deep in the palm, the wrist undercuts it towards the end of the release, and it goes out like a flying saucer. If it lands on the seam, it goes like an offbreak; if it lands on the leather, it goes straight on.

In the orthodox release, the seam points diagonally towards leg slip for a right-hand batter, which gives you both turn and bounce. In this straighter delivery, the seam is parallel. The problem I encountered initially with this ball was that my wrist would tend to push it wider. So I started aiming at the leg stump, but that is not the ideal way to do it. Then I learned the role of the left arm. I began using my left arm to close myself off.

Raman's prodding turns out to be helpful, and I begin to understand the impact of small changes. I am also easily bored trying to bowl the same ball all day. So I keep working with different things, but without moving away from 'there and thereabouts'.

The other trick, especially against left-hand batters, is to use the shiny side of the ball. And not just the ball but also the shiny side of the seam. Once the ball has been used for a while, teams keep shining one side by rubbing it on their pants. In the process, half the seam of the ball also becomes shinier than the other.

When I bowl with a relatively new ball, I keep the shiny side away from the left-hand batter when trying to bowl the regulation offbreak. However, when I hold the shiny side inside, even with the seam pointing towards the slip, the ball first drifts in, then lands on the rough part of the seam and keeps going straight on. The offbreak keeps the outside edge in play, and this delivery either induces the inside edge or gets me the lbw.

Apart from these, another mode of dismissal I have begun to rely on is the catch at short midwicket. Part of it is about having the right field. As Badri knows by now, I am not orthodox with my field. I like my mid-on back because it takes away the release shot. If the batter needs to hit a boundary, they must go across the line now. Besides, I trust the revolutions I put on the ball and the bounce I get. I trust myself to challenge batters so that they can't push me down the ground for three singles in an over because one of the balls is bound to fall out of their reach, turn in, and lob to short midwicket for a catch.

Other modes of dismissal just happen by themselves if I do these things right. If I put a plug on the scoring for long enough, they will have to play a risky shot. That creates chances of the bowled, the stumping or the catch in the outfield. Intercepting that kind of response is also a skill, which I believe I will keep honing. Instinctively, I do tend to know when someone is going to go after me, when someone is going to sweep, or when they are going to use their feet.

* * *

The reflection period is too painful. I enjoy my bowling so much, but being unable to play makes me restless. In a couple of weeks, I want to start bowling in the state nets, reasoning that it is the non-bowling wrist that is injured. Everyone asks me not to be ridiculous. I miss the entire Ranji season. I make my comeback for Jolly Rovers in the second week of January, around Pongal.

I immediately get five wickets, but India Pistons take a one-run lead. In the second innings, when I am batting, I play two lovely flicks for four. Then C. Ganapathy shortens his length, and I go back and punch it ferociously, aiming at the cover gap. However, the ball hits the middle of the bat and still hits the leg stump. It turns out that whenever I am trying to extend my arms to play a shot, my left wrist flips. If it is within my body, I can time a shot, but whenever I need to extend, I get no power into the shot, even though I have been cleared clinically.

My Ranji season may be over, but the selectors reward me by picking me for the South Zone in the Duleep Trophy. That's like being told you are one of the 75 best cricketers in the country outside the internationals.

I get two games in the Duleep Trophy. The bowling is okay, but I really struggle with the bat. The two big Bengal quicks, Ranadeb Bose and Shib Shankar Paul, take me to school on a spicy Wankhede pitch. I even get out hit-wicket when trying to cut Tushar Saha, a left-arm medium bowler. For the next month or so, I take underarm throws and hit them with only my left hand, every day, hundreds of times a day, just to get the strength and the form back.

While we play the Duleep Trophy at Wankhede Stadium, an auction is taking place at a hotel not far away in South Bombay. The BCCI has launched the Indian Premier League, which is its response to the ICL. They are now auctioning the rights to own each of the eight teams. India Cements, patrons of cricket in Chennai, win the Chennai franchise and name it Chennai Super Kings.

I enjoyed the first season of the ICL because it had taken the game to the next level. G. Vignesh, who wasn't getting many opportunities here, was opening the innings and hitting the leather off the ball. Michael Bevan, Inzamam-ul-Haq, Saqlain Mushtaq and Stuart Law—it had been fun to watch them all again.

So, I am really excited about the IPL. An auction takes place for players in February. CSK's strategy is interesting: while other teams pick an icon player, they forego the icon and save that money to splurge on Dhoni in the auction. There can be no bigger icon for me: big hitter, cool finisher, T20 World Cup-winning captain. I really want to play for CSK, but people tell me they have picked Muthiah Muralidaran at the auction. Why would they go for another offspinner?

I return to club cricket in Madras, but I also simultaneously try to find a way to get in touch with those responsible for picking players outside the auction. V.B. Chandrasekar, the selector who picked me for Tamil Nadu, is CSK's man. I widen my net. I make a call to Avinash Vaidya at Royal Challengers, Bangalore, and ask a *Deccan Chronicle* reporter to put my name forward to the person making these calls for Hyderabad.

On the last day before the signing window, I am playing the quarter-final of the 50-over first-division tournament for Jolly Rovers against Globe Trotters, the team owned by MRF. I run into Bharath Reddy here. He says he has seen me bowl in the earlier stages of the tournament, bowling yorkers and being economical. He asks me if I have been picked for an IPL side yet. He has clearly touched a raw nerve, and I start telling him how unfair it is that no team has selected me for the IPL.

Bharath Reddy tells me I will be very good at T20. He asks why I'm not trying for the ICL. I tell him, 'With due respect, sir, I am ready to play the IPL, not the ICL. I love watching the ICL, but I don't want to lose a chance of playing for India.'

We go on to win the quarter-final, then the semi-final, and guess who the final is against? It's Vijay Cricket Club, the team owned by India Cements, who also own CSK. We lose the toss, but bowling first, I take five wickets to set up an easy chase.

Being the final, there is a proper presentation ceremony after the match. Kris Srikkanth, who is also the brand ambassador of CSK, is there to give away the Player-of-the-Match trophy, which goes to me. Now N. Srinivasan, the managing director of India Cements, is also the BCCI president, so the cricketing matters of India Cements are looked at by Kasi Viswanathan, a firm, practical and loyal man. He is at the presentation, too.

Srikkanth is a gregarious person, but he is also a little absent-minded in a cute way. However, he also keeps his ear to the ground through Aniruddha. Every time I run into him, he tells me Ani has good things to say about my cricket. So, in his typical absent-minded fashion, Srikkanth tells me after giving me the trophy, 'Hey, good opportunity for you at CSK. Learn as much as you can. I look forward to working with cricketers like you from Tamil Nadu.'

I stare blankly at him in awkward silence. He stares back at me. Then he looks left and right, and catches the eye of Kasi, who is witnessing this exchange. 'Oh, you haven't picked him?' Srikkanth says, and then adds, 'Suit yourselves.'

The following day, the same cousin who called me after VB had picked me for Tamil Nadu calls to inform me that VB has asked me to report at the CSK office, which is basically the old India Cements office in Tarapore Towers. 'They want to offer you a contract.'

Anirudha and I show up, we sign our contracts, and then VB gives us a glorious speech on what a huge opportunity this is. 'You guys will rub shoulders with the likes of Michael Hussey, M.S. Dhoni, Matthew Hayden and Muralidaran.'

I listen to it earnestly but also think to myself, 'I am not here to rub shoulders with them. I am here to show that I belong here.'

8

The IPL is unlike any cricket I've ever been part of. When we report for the preparatory camp—largely filled with uncapped players because the international stars will arrive two days before the season after fulfilling their international commitments—each one of us is given a new Nokia phone and prepaid Aircel SIM cards with a credit of Rs 10,000. We hear one team has even been given iPhones, and another team has received Xbox units.

There are only ten to twelve of us, but Kepler Wessels, the coach, is here. We train at VB's Nest, Chandasekar's ground. I come across Manpreet Gony, this big fast bowler from Punjab. He is quick. VB has spotted him and is quite impressed with his skills. VB has always been great at spotting talent. I bat and bowl quite well. I think Kepler, at least, is impressed.

Everyone tells me not to expect to play in the first season, which is quite reasonable, but inside my head, I've impressed people in practice games, so I have a chance. 'Don't delude yourself; you'll mostly be a nets bowler,' I am told.

When I bowled at the nets for the ODI between India and West Indies, I was disappointed not because of the international cricketers but because my perception and expectations of them were different from what they were in real life. Now, at CSK, I am not just bowling to them but also sharing the dressing room with them. We have Dhoni, Hussey, Hayden, Murali, Fleming, Oram and Raina among other stars.

With Hayden, there is no such disappointment. I have a certain image of Hayden in mind: a confident, boisterous, brutish person. A day before our first match of the IPL, in Mohali against Kings XI Punjab, Kepler opens the floor to the players to speak. 'Haydos' is the first one to speak. He says, 'Sreesanth and Brett Lee will come running at me. They will try to shape the ball back into me to try and knock me over. But I'm going to just walk straight at them and try to go right over their heads. And I'm going to go really hard. They will come at me, but I will be nasty to them. I will show them who is the boss.'

I have never seen such confidence. I have not even seen really high-scoring T20 games so far. Later in the night, Brendon McCullum gets the IPL off to a glittering start with 158, but for me, the real stuff happens at 4 p.m. the next day. MS wins the toss, Haydos goes out to bat, and he immediately walks straight at Lee and slams him over midwicket.

Huss, true to his image of being low-key, smart, grounded and humble, quietly scores a hundred after Haydos gives us that start. A winning start.

Just before the next match, in Chennai, Haydos declares again: 'I am going to take Shaun Pollock down. First over mid-on. He gets annoyed whenever I do that. Then he will bowl a slower ball, and I will sweep him over fine leg.'

In a corner, I'm thinking, 'This is Shaun Pollock he is talking about, right?' The next day, Haydos goes out and puts Pollock on the roof of the Madras Cricket Club, breaking a couple of roof tiles. As promised, he sweeps him over fine leg too. I am in the dugout, and I'm getting goosebumps watching it.

I really enjoy watching Haydos operate. I find myself attracted to his style of play, his way of speaking, and his way of going about business. He is the one I relate to the most.

Off the field, Haydos is a chilled-out person. He is here with his family and spends a lot of time with his daughter, Grace, near the hotel swimming pool. It is a luxury for me. Both the swimming pool, coming from first-class cricket, and also Haydos's company. I hesitate to speak with him; I wait for him to finish whatever he is doing and then introduce myself. He is extremely friendly. I ask him all kinds of questions, and he patiently answers. I suspect he enjoys having conversations.

How do you deal with pressure? How do you face Murali? How do you stand at slip for Shane Warne? I've watched you take some great catches; what is your mindset at slips?

I remember Haydos sweeping a lot during the great Border-Gavaskar Trophy of 2000–01. I ask him how he started sweeping. What his mindset is. Whether he picks the line, whether he picks the length, or if he goes by the trajectory. And he says it's none of those; he has certain passages of play. That he picks his time for the sweep, which would be early on in a bowler's spell. Just to try and throw off the bowler.

Haydos tells me that Harbhajan Singh didn't enjoy bowling around the wicket. He bowled a lot from over. So, he felt that whenever he bowled over the wicket, the sweep shot was almost there for the taking. And that whenever Murali bowled the *doosra*, the line changed distinctly.

These are great insights for me as an offspinner. I used to think Harbhajan had a great angle on him while getting it to spin from over the wicket. He, on the other hand, sees it as a free hit because it is almost impossible to get him lbw from over the wicket. It is fascinating to learn the rationale behind the way he bats.

Haydos has wide interests in life outside of cricket. Still, when he returns to the game, he plays it hard. I try to become like him and maintain interests outside cricket, which, in my case, are movies. I wait for Haydos to turn up at the nets so I can bowl to him.

Just as I was told, I don't get to play a match in the first season, but I bowl a lot in the nets at Flem, Oram, Haydos and Huss. Apart from Haydos, I look forward to bowling to Huss, but he is there only for a part of the season as he needs to return to international cricket.

My biggest early realization about T20 cricket is that the ball doesn't really get old in 20 overs. At club cricket or first-class cricket, I hardly get access to new balls. Not regularly at any rate. Bowling with the old ball, I know it is easy to restrict batters because the old white ball starts to rag. T20 is going to be different for spinners.

At CSK, we fortunately get a couple of dozen balls for every nets session. I go through a couple of new balls every session myself. One to start off the session, and the second when it becomes difficult for the batter to hit.

I start picking up on cues such as: When are a certain batter's initial moments if he's looking to sweep? What sort of adjustments do they make when they try to play a big shot? What are the differences? How are they playing? How are they positioning themselves when they're trying to take a single? I sharpen that awareness through the season.

I more than hold my own in the nets. I keep beating them, nicking them off, and hitting them in front. It gives me a lot of confidence because these are the kind of batters I will encounter in international cricket. The skill level or attitude of the others in international cricket will not be too different. It is a great feeling to know that I can beat them, that I can get them out, that I can hang in there, that I will probably be good at international cricket, and that I belong here.

* * *

One place I don't belong is at the IPL after-match parties. It is intimidating to go in. Apart from the two teams that have played, the who's-who of the city hosting the match is often there. Everyone is glamorous. The way they dress, the way they move around, I know they must be big to have been invited here. I feel like the kid I was outside Not Just Jazz By the Bay in Bombay. 'What if I end up eating something I can't pay for?' The adult version of that kid.

Even if I muster up the courage and smoothness to hang out with the glamorous people, the sheer number of unknown people intimidates me. I am outspoken when it comes to cricket. If someone asks me about the game earlier in the day, even if cursorily, it is enough of a trigger to launch me into a full-blown analysis of the match. I am not good at assessing people and knowing what to say to whom. You never know who is who, and what my saying 'this could have been done differently' can be construed as. These are not Raman and Badri we are speaking of, although Badri is part of the squad.

Besides, my hands are full with cricket and college. I have never been to a nightclub. If you say party, to me, it means a birthday party or a wedding. This is a completely different universe. Out of curiosity, once in a while, I stand outside the party to see what goes on there. More so because actors Vijay and Nayanthara are CSK's brand ambassadors, and they drop in for a while. Other than that, I use the time to study. I still need a degree name to go up on the nameplate in my head.

That nameplate situation is momentarily resolved at the end of the IPL when I am offered a job at India Cements. I am now 'R. Ashwin, Senior Manager, Costs Department, India Cements'. Costs is the department where all cricketers patronized by India Cements laze around. To get here, I have to switch clubs and end a memorable association with Chemplast. Nobody at Chemplast begrudges the move because they know India Cements owns the IPL team for which I play. This only makes my future prospects brighter. Now, I play for Vijay Cricket Club.

* * *

Tamil Nadu. India Under-17. CSK. Jolly Rovers. Alwarpet CC. Vijay CC. None of these is my favourite team. RUCA is the love of my life. Ramakrishnapuram Underarm Cricket Association. We have come up with a name for our team because we are hosting a tournament in our street: the West Mambalam Premier League (WMPL).

We've printed pamphlets and flyers, and we stick them in any shop that will let us. The WMPL is played in the front yard by 110 teams of four players each in two categories. It's not quite a yard; it's a corridor that runs alongside the house. These are four-over matches with an over each of batting powerplay and bowling powerplay. Normally, the field of play includes a bowler, a fielder and a batter. The umpire perches himself on the boundary wall behind the bowler. During the batting powerplay, there is no fielder allowed. During the bowling powerplay, all three fielders are allowed inside. A wide ball is not just an extra run; the next ball is a free hit.

We have three teams ourselves: RUCA Juniors, RUCA Seniors A and RUCA Seniors B. We are unbeatable in this tournament. Not only are we the hosts, but we have mastered the tricks needed here. Bhuvnesh wears Bermuda shorts to these matches to be able to catch ferocious hits in the loose cloth between his legs. We know the exact trajectory at which the ball clears the boundary wall, in which case the batter is out. It's a little like a tennis player on the net knowing which balls will fly out of the court.

Tamil Nadu Ranji and Under-19 players have also tried their hand. H. Gopinath is one of them. We still keep winning. The semi-finals and finals are played under lights—temporary halogen lamps set up by me. It is even covered in the *Deccan Chronicle*.

We also play 14-over tennis-ball matches in parks all over Chennai. Appa has taught me how to swing the tennis ball. You bowl a lot of yorkers with the tennis ball, but the batters still hit it pretty hard. As the ball keeps getting hit, the fur or feathers on the tennis ball start to come up. So you pull it up a touch more on one side. Then, if you sling it with a low arm, the ball swings beautifully.

We have also started our own ingenious style of ball-tampering. When you go to these 14-over matches, you have to bring your own ball. The new ball, though, is nice and fluffy. It doesn't bounce, it doesn't fizz through, it doesn't swing, and the *sodakku* doesn't sit in the surface. So, we actually burn the ball before the day of the match. Wrap it in a newspaper and actually put it on fire.

It comes out charred black, and then we hit it a few times to knock off the carbon. It loses its fluffiness, and it becomes easier to lift feathers on one side. We also keep it in the fridge overnight and wipe all the moisture out in the morning with a towel. It still looks like a new ball, but it isn't. I have a suspicion we are not the only team that does it. Teams that don't tamper get walloped. When we go to bigger tournaments, the balls are provided by the organisers. There, we have to contend with just the lifting of the fur.

Cosco is such a ubiquitous brand that tennis balls used for cricket are known as Cosco balls. However, we like playing with Mercury or Penn. The Penn has less fur, so it is easier to get rid of the fluffiness.

* * *

CSK lose to the Rajasthan Royals in the final of the IPL. I have been released after seven to eight games, but Manpreet Gony is our breakthrough star. He has played just one season of domestic cricket, but he is part of the Indian team for the Asia Cup in Pakistan.

In the Asia Cup, I watch another young man bowl the *sodakku* to devastating effect. I immediately recognize him. Years ago, in a camp in Chennai, former India spinner V.V. Kumar told this Sri Lankan kid in front of me to develop a stock ball. It is hard to tell what his stock ball still is, but he is running through the sides. Nobody seems to have a response for Ajantha Mendis. Sri Lanka even bench him for the league game against India because they don't want India to be prepared for what will hit them in the final.

India are 76 for 1 in nine overs and chasing 274 when Mendis is introduced. He runs through the batting with six wickets of sheer wizardry. In the next month, Mendis follows it up with 26 wickets in three Tests against India. Mendis bowls the *sodakku* much more frequently than Rangana Herath did when we were in Sri Lanka for the MJ Gopalan Trophy. I am interested to see if he will be easier to pick because of that. The *sodakku* now has a universal English name too: the carrom ball. It makes sense too: it is like flicking the carrom striker with one finger. Clearly, Mendis didn't take VV's advice years back at the spinners' camp in Chennai.

I feel restless. That it has taken me so long to start working on this delivery when I have been bowling it for years with the tennis ball. I now know I have to work even harder to master it with the cricket ball because I know the impact it can have. I am looking forward to the next season all the more now.

9

I've been practising yoga for a year now. Not to tackle my restlessness but because my body is a little out of proportion. My limbs are disproportionately long, and my upper body is disproportionately short, making it impossible for me to sit upright on the floor. I am sure it has some impact on overall fitness, too.

I find a yoga guru, Venkat Sir, in Ashok Nagar, which is about 2 km from home. Venkat Sir leaves his home for mine at 4.30 a.m., and we do yoga from 5 a.m. to 6.30 a.m. *Padmasana* is still impossible for me, but I am now able to sit in *sukhasana*. Both poses involve sitting cross-legged on the floor, but in *padmasana*, the feet cross each other to end up on the thighs.

Yoga is not a substitute for conventional training, but it complements my other fitness work beautifully. I have started to lose weight; I don't feel as heavy as I used to, and I am more mobile on the field.

On this one day, in the initial stages of the 2008–09 season, Venkat sir asks me to get into *savasana*, which literally means to lie down like a dead body. Once I have relaxed in that posture, he asks me to feel my breath go through my body, starting from the toes through the calf, knees and groin, all the way to the top. He is putting me in *yoga nidra*, a yogic sleep or deeply meditative state.

Then Venkat sir suddenly tells me, 'You are now in the middle of Chepauk Stadium. You are bowling from the D Stand End.

102

Now, you have picked up the first wicket. Imagine how you took the wicket. Now, the next batter is under pressure. Now, you are getting the second wicket. Then imagine the third and the fourth, completely surrendering yourself. Then the eighth, the ninth and the tenth. All 10 are yours.'

I wasn't expecting this, but I begin visualizing every wicket: catches at short leg, catches at slip and carrom balls. When he says I have picked all 10, I briefly smile. Then he says, 'Now you can turn to your right, and whenever you are comfortable, open your eyes and get up.'

After our session, I have to go to captain Tamil Nadu Under-22 against Hyderabad Under-22 at Chepauk. I also have to drop Amma off at work on the way. I am in a kind of daze. On the car radio, I hear the news of the team selection for the upcoming Challenger Trophy, a one-day tournament played by three teams called India Red, Blue and Green. S. Badrinath from Tamil Nadu is going to captain one of the sides.

I am still in a sort of meditative state when a car from behind bumps into us. Amma tells me not to fight. We can claim insurance. I drop her and go to the ground. It starts raining, as it often does in October in Madras. It is a pitch expected to help spinners, but this rain could make it tacky and help spinners even on Day 1.

I lose the toss, and Hyderabad choose to bat. I bring myself on towards the end of the first hour and start picking up wickets. One, two, three, four, five and six. All six to me. During the tea break, it hits me. 'Will it actually come true? Is it going to come true?'

Now I am thinking of what Venkat sir told me in the morning. I am thinking of what an achievement it will be to take it all then. I don't get any more wickets in the innings. I take seven more in the second innings as we win comfortably.

After the match, I tell Venkat sir what happened. He asks me for a more detailed description. Once I tell him everything, he says that until the tea break, I had surrendered myself completely. The moment I began thinking of all 10 wickets, I stopped staying in the moment. 'I am not saying it would have happened had you not thought of it,' he tells me. 'But it might have happened.'

Venkat sir goes on to explain that my job is quite meditative. When I am playing cricket, I must be completely immersed in the game. I must accept what is happening and stay immersed in the activity. I find it all hard to fathom.

What I can definitely understand is that Badri is not the only one from Tamil Nadu going to the Challenger Trophy. I am going too. I am one of the 45 best limited-over cricketers outside the senior India team. In fact, some of the first-choice players are playing too, as there is no international cricket taking place. I am part of the Blue team, which is led by Yuvraj Singh and has, among others, Robin Uthappa, Virat Kohli, Irfan Pathan, Dinesh Karthik and Ajinkya Rahane. I take eight wickets in three matches as we stay unbeaten and lift the trophy. Among my victims are Rohit Sharma, Cheteshwar Pujara and S. Badrinath.

The biggest wicket, though, is Yusuf Pathan, who is on a rampage, and nobody wants to bowl to him. I snatch the ball from Yuvraj and get Yusuf out, caught and bowled. After the match, Yuvraj tells me he has never seen a spinner with such a big heart.

* * *

Come Ranji Trophy time, I am reunited with the 'there and thereabouts' of W.V. Raman. There are two non-negotiables with Raman: as an offspinner, you cannot get cut, and you cannot get driven through the covers. Even when I take five or six wickets, he talks to me about how I got cut off a certain ball. He never talks about the times someone hits me for a six or sweeps me or slog-sweeps, but the cut and the cover-drive are just not acceptable to him.

Raman always says, 'As an offspinner, you just cannot be cut or driven through covers. If someone is looking to hit you there, they must risk their wicket.'

Now that is a generic statement. *How* do I make them risk their wicket? That is something I need to figure out. Quite literally, it means you don't bowl short, and you don't bowl too full. If a batter is driving, they must have to reach for it. It sounds good, but it is not possible to be that precise with length through the day.

I start to think of Raman's words as a captain. I have captained enough at junior levels. As a captain, it starts to make more sense to me: I don't want my spinner to err both on length *and* line, nor do I want to be defending both sides of the field.

As a captain, I have nine fielders to play with. Perennially, there will be one fewer fielder on one side of the pitch. For offspinners, we often have four on the off side and five on the leg side. There is a slip for the catch. The point is in place to deny the single to that one ball that goes straight on and gets a thick outside edge. The cover is there to deny the single to a check-drive when the batter doesn't quite reach the pitch of the ball. The mid-off is there to prevent the batter from playing inside-out to a slightly fuller, straighter ball and getting off-strike.

These are fielders for good balls, not for bad balls or extraordinary shots. These fielders are there to create pressure by denying them risk-free runs. Now you can get cover-driven without risk only if you bowl too full and too wide. If you do go full, you ensure you stay at around the fourth stump because then the batter has to play to the leg side.

This is what I understand from Raman's words. Your first job as a bowler is to provide control. The yardstick for a bowler's performance can't be wickets because there are only 10, and you can't get a five-wicket haul every day, unlike batters, who don't have to share a certain number of runs. The yardstick has to be whether you have been able to control the game or whether the team has been in the game and been able to exercise control over an extended period of time.

Apparently, the classic way of bowling offspin is to bowl it wide, drift it away beautifully, create a gap between the bat and pad, and then either go through the gap or get the bat-pad catch. It sounds good on paper or coming out of the mouths of coaches and commentators, but out there on the pitch, it doesn't work.

Pitches in India tend to lose life on the final two days. Even when it turns, it doesn't fizz off the surface, giving batters time to recover. We don't even have a left-arm fast bowler to create rough for me. On the first two days, anyway, it sits up nicely for them to go back and cut me.

And there are some ruthless players of spin going around. If I bowl that poetic line, Shiv Sundar Das will cut me for six boundaries in an over, from third man to either side of cover. And getting cut is totally unacceptable. Mithun Manhas, Halhadar Das, Robin Uthappa, Yere Goud, Rajat Bhatia and Sanjay Bangar are all unforgiving to spinners. In our nets, we have our captain Badri and veteran S. Sharath, who give me great practice.

There was this Ranji Trophy one-day game against Andhra in 2007 where I started off with my usual off-side ring. Batters began to lap-sweep me. For a moment, I didn't know how to react. I had never been lap-swept before. So, Raman told me to get an extra fielder on the leg side and bowl straighter lines.

Once I started to get it right with tighter lines in 50-over cricket, I tried it at the start of the next first-class season on a dead Chennai track against Maharashtra, who had Kedar Jadhav and Venugopal Rao. I bowled 50 overs at 2.5 an over and picked up six wickets.

By the end of the 2008–09 Ranji season, I've fine-tuned the straighter line to the extent that I can actually bowl without a cover when there is a bit of turn on offer, which gives me two extra fielders on the leg side.

Further lessons await in the Duleep Trophy, played between teams from the five zones. We have Rahul Dravid playing for the South Zone. We are playing the Central Zone in Bangalore. I am struggling. I keep missing my length. I kept getting driven. I pick up only one wicket in 26 overs.

Our coach is Vijay Bharadwaj, a former India all-rounder. He tells me that whenever he bowled too full, he would pull his front leg back when delivering the ball.

Before the final in Chennai, I take this thought to Sunil Subramanian. We have a relationship where I bowl a lot at him whenever I am struggling. He is also old-school. He wants me to keep bowling and spin the ball hard. Pulling the front foot back works. I also realize that I might need to work on a completely different action in first-class cricket.

Not that it matters in the final. We are up against a strong West Zone, who have won the toss and are batting. The new ball is in this beautiful fast bowler Sreesanth's hand; Rahul, his former

Test captain, is at slip, and he runs in and bowls legspin second ball. Cut for four.

The same day, with the second new ball, he bowls beautifully, nice areas, gets movement, takes the edge, and Rahul catches it beside his head. And he says, 'Sree, with the second ball you are getting such good carry. What were you doing in the morning?'

* * *

Between the Ranji Trophy and the IPL, Raman rewards me for working things out by myself. I am made the captain of the Ranji Trophy one-day team for the knockouts of the Vijay Hazare Trophy when M. Vijay is called up for the India side. Opening batter Abhinav Mukund is the vice-captain of the side but is not getting any runs.

Just before we leave for Agartala for the matches, a reporter brings up the case of another batter who is sitting out and can also bowl seam-up. That is a rare commodity. I tell him that if Abhi doesn't score runs, he will have to make way. I don't put much thought into it and just say it off the cuff.

Once the article comes out, Raman calls me aside and tells me I cannot say that. I tell him, 'Sir, I just felt like it, but it's not like we're going to drop him.'

Raman explains to me what kind of impact it will have on Abhi. I realize Raman is right, so I immediately go and speak to Abhi. I tell him it's not as though I'm targeting or cornering him. 'I know you are the vice-captain of the side as well. So, I'm sure you will do well. But because he asked me in comparison to the both of you, I just made that statement. I shouldn't have said that. It was wrong on my part,' I say.

I tell Abhi I am happy to retract the statement. Abhi says, 'No, no, it is okay.' It helps that he knows me, as we have played a lot of school cricket together. I know it is not easy to completely take it out of his head, but once we have had that conversation, I go into the matches with a clear head and heart.

Abhi fails in both the quarter-final and the semi-final but we stick with him, and he responds with a century in the final as we lift the trophy. I tell Abhi again, 'I did commit a mistake. It's not like I didn't believe you were capable of this.'

In my heart, I knew I hadn't said the wrong thing, but Raman did me a favour by telling me I shouldn't be saying it in public and that I should, as a captain, consider the impact my words could have on others. Raman has never held back when handling me as a captain.

I was reminded of this time when I was made captain of the TNCA XI for the KSCA All India Invitational Tournament in Bengaluru. These were two-day matches, basically one-innings first-class matches. We had Dr D.Y. Patil Sports Academy at 142 for 9 in the 63rd over. Ryan Ninan was a decent batter, definitely batting too low at No. 9. He and Prashant Bhor, their No. 11, frustrated us. So as soon as the new ball became available, I claimed it because I had L. Balaji.

They only started scoring quicker and played out the next 20 overs, which is when you have to declare an innings closed in these matches. They ended up with 256 for 9. We ended up winning, but Raman told me taking the new ball was the wrong call. And I told him we had them nine down, trusted my seam attack, and they didn't deliver.

Raman said, 'No, you're wrong. Because for a tailender, when the ball is old and slow, it'll be tougher for them. Even if they're not getting out, run scoring will be slower. What you did was absolutely wrong. Own up to your mistake. And do not come and tell me they didn't deliver. If they didn't deliver, you have a part in it.'

After accepting my mistake, I asked Raman, 'Sir, why do you do this? I've never seen you talk like this with Badri in front of a lot of people.'

Raman said, 'You're right. I don't do that with Badri because he's a senior cricketer, he's earned his reputation, he has earned his stripes. And I won't do it. I respect him.'

Then I asked him: 'Sir, so you don't respect me?'

Raman didn't get annoyed at the continued questioning. Instead, he said, 'Of course I respect you, but you don't have to necessarily be a cricketer with that much ego that I have to think twice before talking to you. One of the reasons I picked you as a captain was because I believe you are above a lot of other people in terms of how you judge the game. You come across as someone who will put the game and the situation ahead of himself. And I think you should continue doing that. If the ego kicks in, I'll kick you.'

I file these away among other lessons learnt by being with Raman. The day after the Vijay Hazare final, I receive a congratulatory call from N. Srinivasan, a BCCI office bearer and managing director of India Cements, which owns CSK. I feel that a longer run in the IPL is not far away.

* * *

The IPL in 2009 has been shifted to South Africa because of the general elections in India. Just the fact that I am part of the squad and travelling to South Africa gives me hope that M.S. Dhoni at least knows of my existence now. This is the year he has apparently had conversations with the coaching staff about the depth of the squad and promising players. So I am hoping I will get a game this year.

Another reason for this optimism is that this year CSK is using me for an ad shoot for the clothing brand Peter England. It is an unusual place for an uncapped player to be. After the photo shoot, there is a meet-and-greet programme. It is nerve-wracking to meet strangers, but just before going on stage, I see a face backstage that brings back an old feeling: a sweet flutter in the tummy.

It's Prithi from Hindi class in the eighth standard. She gave me the butterflies then, and she gives me the butterflies now. But I am much more confident now, and immediately rush to talk to her.

'Hey, how are you?' I ask, unable to hide the happiness and surprise on my face.

She has an expression of shock. In a second, I form thought bubbles over her head even as she looks for a response. 'What the hell is this guy doing here?' I imagine her thinking. 'Where has he got this confidence from?'

Before going on stage, I tell her we must catch up. She says sure, but I totally expect her to not follow through with that.

While on stage, I think I must properly ask her out. As soon as I get off stage, I go to her and tell her, 'Look, when we were in school together, I obviously had a crush on you, but then it was different. I didn't have the confidence to properly talk to you, and people would make fun of us. It was always awkward. We only spoke on the phone. I think we must catch up and go out for dinner.'

She agrees in principle and also gives me her number, but we don't have time for a date before the IPL. Off I go to South Africa, looking forward to life both on and off the field.

* * *

One thing I don't look forward to is IPL parties, which get even wilder in South Africa. There is a lot of time and temptation to attend them because I get to play only in our first and last league matches. In the first, on debut, I neither get to bat nor bowl; in the second, I bowl four overs for 13 runs and two wickets on a spinners' track in Durban. We go on to lose the semi-final to Royal Challengers Bangalore in Johannesburg.

I manage to make it to a couple of parties. We are staying at a hotel called Sandton Sun, which is in the middle of a shopping mall. I go to the parties with Palani Amarnath, my Tamil Nadu teammate. During the parties in the evening, the place turns into what looks like a Fashion TV set. There are bouncers outside who tag you in.

Inside, the party is a heaving, throbbing scene. There are glamorous people of different races and ethnicities from all over the world. The bar keeps flowing. I don't drink. I like dancing, but I can't be myself in front of so many people. So we sit in a corner and just watch people. After a while, I get bored and tired, so I go to sleep.

During the rest of the season, I only go to parties when I know that the whole team is going to be there. I prefer to stay in and sleep the rest of the time.

At the nets, I am neither bored nor tired, although I miss Haydos there. He has quit international cricket and domestic cricket, but here he comes—a retired cricketer for all intents and purposes—and smacks fifties in practically every match, batting like a magician. And he hardly turns up for practice. On his days off, he just goes surfing. The IPL is like a break between his surfing escapades. He speaks a lot about having interests outside of cricket. I identify with Haydos. So I take after him and hardly turn up for optional nets sessions.

On one occasion we are checking in at the Sandton Sun, but my luggage hasn't arrived. So, I call up the support staff, who don't sound happy to be called up about the luggage. One of them holds influential posts in Chennai cricket.

At the next nets session, I notice players are staring at me. Palani Amarnath later tells me that my not turning up for optional nets hasn't sat well with the team. 'With whom exactly?' I ask. 'Did MS say anything?'

'No,' says Palani, 'But others are. They are saying if we non-international players don't come for optional nets, how will Mahi see us?'

I immediately realize the said member of the support staff is trying to put me in my place. I tell Palani I am a hard-working cricketer and will not have my commitment questioned. I say to Palani but loud enough for the member of the support staff to hear, 'If Mahi has to see me only on optional practice days and pick me, I don't want to get picked. If it is mandatory for me to come, why call it optional practice?'

I know this, too, will be narrated to MS. Then I try to put myself in MS's shoes. If I am the captain, and somebody has uncharitable things to say about one of my players, I will first wonder what this person would have said for the player to react that way. I will give the benefit of the doubt to the player.

However, I am not sure how MS will actually respond. Or the ten other people to whom the incident might have been narrated.

Optional or not, I don't want to miss any practice that Haydos is coming to. Every time Haydos turns up for the nets, he finds me waiting to bowl at him. Even when he hits me, I find something to learn. I find Michael Hussey tougher to bowl to. With Haydos, I can sense he is about to sweep, chip-and-charge, or play some other big shot. With Huss, I know his go-to shots are the slog-sweep and the chip over extra cover, but I can never predict when he will do that. He's this fox that is waiting and ready to strike at the right time.

Neither of them is quite the nightmare that MS is in the nets. Back at Chepauk, our nets are out on the main square. The number of times I have seen him hit Muthiah Muralidaran out of the stadium is unreal. He is a proper terror. Every time he steps out, it is a six, no matter what you do.

I like to challenge myself against MS not just because he murders spin but also because he is the captain and I need to impress him as I am not getting regular games. I try to bowl yorkers to contain him. I keep changing my line to try to beat him when he steps out.

During a nets session, I bowl the *sodakku*, by now known everywhere as carrom ball, to MS. He defends it back and immediately asks me, 'Did you bowl the carrom ball?' I nod. Then he asks me what field I would have if I were to bowl it in a match. I tell him the field, and he nods and goes back to batting.

So every time I bowl the carrom ball, I ask him if he picked it. And if he picked it, at what point did he pick it? Was it when I was loading? Did he spot any tells, or did he pick it up upon release? When it comes to cricket, I am basically made of questions. MS doesn't discourage me and answers every question sincerely. He never brings up the optional nets either.

* * *

We return to India on 25 May, a day before Prithi's birthday this time— 26 May. This time I don't have to call their home to get through her to wish her. Now I have her mobile number. When I call her to wish her, her response is better than ever. So, I keep in touch with her. I keep texting her, but she keeps giving me what feels like the cold shoulder. Then suddenly, days after I've texted, she responds, and we start chatting. Then she goes silent for days with no response to my texts.

I am unable to figure out our situation, but I ask her out to dinner on various occasions. She says sure, but never gets around to making time. So whenever she responds to texts, I keep asking her about the dinner, but she neither says no nor comes around to actually going. I, in the words of W.V. Raman, keep staying there or thereabouts.

Later in the year, I buy a new car out of the IPL money—a Honda City. I am driving and suddenly find an excuse to call Prithi to wish her for a made-up day. After wishing her, I ask her where she is. She says 10D, short for the restaurant 10 Downing Street, for an office event. I happen to be around 10D, and I offer her a lift home.

We have a nice chat on the way home, even though it is just a ten-minute drive. By the end of it, I finally have what I think is a date in a few days. We go for a meal to Tuscana, the pizzeria in Adyar. We have a great time, but I don't think she is ready to be in a relationship with me yet. We stay in touch on and off—the odd dinner and long conversations on the phone—but we don't really know where this is headed. I am sure I am madly in love, so I continue to wait for Prithi to be sure of it.

* * *

I may have to wait for Prithi, but I am ready to move to third base and beyond with the other love of my life, RUCA, which can mean only one thing: take this motley crew to cricket-ball matches. We retain the name RUCA even though it expands to Ramakrishnapuram Underarm Cricket Association. I coach them and play for them whenever I am in town. Here's our beloved team.

Raju. He wrote India on his body in blood and also asked his girlfriend to feel the *kumkum* being applied to her forehead over the phone. He lives in Ashok Nagar, a five-minute drive or a twelve-minute run away. He is my cousin's friend from school. He wants to learn cricket from me. He comes on his bike but is often late and thus gets to bat last. So, he makes his parents move to a house right opposite ours just to be able to play on our street. He calls himself a medium-pacer but floats gentle outswingers.

What Raju lacks in skill, he makes up for in passion. He truly believes he can play for India. He can hit the ball big, but if you bowl straight at him, his feet get in a tangle, and he gets out lbw.

Even when I am not there, he comes home with the rest of the team to play. He constantly wants me to help him sort out the lbw problem. When I am not there, he gets me on Skype and places the laptop there as he plays.

I tell him to watch Graeme Smith, as he doesn't have an off-side game. 'Just open your stance and play everything to leg like Smith does. Your front leg is going right across because you are looking to play into the off side.'

Once I am back, I am eager to see how he bats. So now he shuffles to off to try to hit to leg and manages to get his front leg out of the way but gets hit on the back leg. Out lbw again. That's a problem we're never able to solve.

Raju is my favourite on the team because of his intent and passion. I even make him captain of the team, whereupon he refuses to listen to anyone but me. During matches, he wears Bluetooth headphones to consult with me—our very own Bob Woolmer–Hansie Cronje moment.

Bhuvnesh. King of street cricket. Of long Bermuda shorts fame to easily catch balls in them. He is not a fan of Raju because I have made him captain. Bhuvan can't run fast because of an issue with his feet, nor is he agile. So we make him the wicketkeeper.

I even get him MS's used gloves and pads. He is so inspired that he changes his Facebook profile name to MS Bhuvnesh and uses MS's photo as his display picture. He doesn't stop there. Next, he changes his name to Brendon Bhuvnesh and uses McCullum's picture.

Bhuvan is a master organizer. He talks to the opposition to settle on bet money and determines and marks the boundaries with stones or rags lying around. He is eventually made our captain.

As captain, Bhuvan makes sure to place slips next to him because he just loves to collect the ball and nonchalantly toss it to the slips the way wicketkeepers in international cricket do. The slips then pass the ball along to the bowler. Never mind that just his collecting the ball cleanly is an event worthy of celebration by itself, which is probably why he keeps appealing every time, annoying not just the opposition and the umpires but also us.

Soon, he introduces a legspinner into the attack and calls in a slip again just so that he can toss the ball stylishly. With spinners, though, it is an even rarer event for him to collect the ball because once he goes down in his squat, his feet get locked and he can't get up. So, most of the time, he collects the ball in front of his face and tosses it to the slip. Not to forget the annoying appeal in between.

This one ball Bhuvan doesn't see at all, and it bursts through his hands and hits him in the nose. I am at cover, and I see blood ooze almost like those fire hydrants in Hollywood movies when cars hit them. There is blood on his shirt, on the ground and even on the stumps. It is a moment of serious concern, but everyone, including the umpires, is on the floor, howling with laughter.

Shyam. My cousin. Raju's friend. He has a weird batting technique, but he can somehow score 20 runs. Anything but a cricketer, he finds ways to be effective. He just puts his front leg outside the leg stump and hits down the ground. Even if the ball is coming at his face, he clears the front leg and tries to hit it down the ground. It's not really technique but self-preservation because he is afraid of the cricket ball.

Shyam calls himself Peter Siddle, but he runs in and bowls googlies. He once bowls a 28-ball over. We start calling him Peter Schedule because we have to clear our schedules whenever he bowls.

We pay Rs 12,000 to enter a tournament where the prize money is Rs 3 lakh. The movie *Chennai 600028* is still fresh in our memories. It is also based on street cricketers. In our minds, we are in a movie.

It rains the night before our first match. The ground has, of course, not dried properly, so as the coach, I start giving the boys catching practice. Bhuvan, as usual, takes the catches and tosses the ball to the side. To Shyam, I am giving these high catches, and every time he catches, he wrings his hands because he feels the pain. He drops two or three, and I get really upset. He commits fully to the next one, which is a really high ball. He gets under it, but at the last moment, his fear wins, and he pulls his hands away. For the first time ever, I see a cricketer getting injured on the toe when taking a high catch and the ball flies to the adjacent tennis courts.

Sai Kumar. Proper corporate guy. Everything about him is proper. He wears crisp, spotless whites, comes in a wide-brim hat, carries a full kitbag with GM pads and a Gray Nicolls bat, but can't play to save his life. Loves Harsha Bhogle, speaks cricket like him.

For four years, he has duped us with fake scorecards. Whenever we challenge his cricketing credentials, he comes back with a copy of the scorecard for the match he played for his other team, the Silver Foxes. On those scorecards, he has always scored a hundred. One day, we notice there are two Sais on these scorecards, and we immediately know it is some other Sai's hundred that our Sai is taking credit for.

When we lose two or three games in a row, Sai gloats that he will bring a player called Raj Kumar from the Silver Foxes, who is a 'handy all-rounder', the 'Jacques Kallis' of their team. We think, 'Wow, now we will have a gun for hire.' Come match day, Raj Kumar turns out to be worse than the player he replaces.

Another time, we enter a league called CSCA, which is run by this guy called Richard. The entry fee is Rs 30,000, with a guarantee of a minimum of seven matches. It turns out later that it is not actually a league and Richard is just organizing social matches with other teams, who also think they are in a league. Sometimes we're playing a quarter-final, but the other team thinks they're playing the final. Sometimes, we run into the same team again, and we are both told that we've made the knockouts. In reality, the amount we have paid is to organize grounds, umpires and balls, and also to get us a team to play against every weekend.

On this one weekend, Sai is given out lbw. He walks back, abusing the umpire. Because he has introduced us to Richard through his corporate circles, he holds influence with him. So even before the new batter comes in, Sai asks for the phone and calls Richard.

'Hey Richard, where did you get the umpires from? You need to get ICC-standard umpires.'

As we are laughing on the sidelines, Sai goes to the leg umpire, who has no way to adjudicate on the lbw, and browbeats him into telling Richard he was not out. The other umpire, though, stands his ground. Sai has to eventually walk off.

Vicky. Bhuvnesh's younger brother. Stays in big brother's shadow. Committed and skilled cricketer, solid fielder, one of the best we have seen. He can take catches running back with ease. His batting is not natural, but he is eventually promoted to the top order.

Vicky is a great observer. He picks on the tiniest of details and makes fun of everyone. His neighbour is Raju, who wants to play for India but is too lazy. Even after moving to our street, he is late for the 4 p.m. start. Vicky goes to his house to call him and finds him sleeping on a slanting bed. Vicky pushes him down along the slope and asks him, 'Are you imagining playing at Lord's? Is that why you are sleeping on a slope to get acclimatized to the slope at Lord's?'

Sriram. My other cousin, brother of Shyam, who was gifted but was never allowed to play with the cricket ball. Lives in his own daze. Has lost his fitness, and now, he just comes and executes his skill without moving much.

Aravind Srinivas. He is Raju's friend, but also his downfall. Raju has introduced Aravind to our team, but Aravind shares with us all the weird things Raju does. He is a seam bowler but has an unnecessarily long and slow run-up. We tell Aravind and Raju that even though the two of them are friends, they can't both kill us with their slow 'fast' bowling. One of them must become an offspinner.

Aravind idolizes Graeme Swann, so he becomes an offspinner. Very smart and intelligent, he goes on to play league cricket and even picks up a few five-fors. His low fitness and lack of strength get in the way of higher honours.

Vivek. A failed professional cricketer. He has played for the Jolly Rovers. His highest score is zero not out, and his lowest is duck out. He is still a level above RUCA's cricket and our opponents. He scores more runs than I do, and also bowls good legspin.

Rama. A reasonably talented right-arm fast bowler. He stays with us and improves remarkably. Again, a committed cricketer. He can come in at noon and start knocking or bowling.

Manu. A very talented legspinner. Just like his variations, it is hard to tell what he says is truth and what is fabrication. And truth is the variation and not the stock ball.

Another Sriram. Nicknamed Vendu Murugan, the popular comedy character played by the legendary Vadivelu. Wears thick, soda-bottle glasses. He sees Rama and wants to emulate him. Always the team man: running drinks, fielding as a substitute and still there for every match. If we lose a game, he is disappointed because he believes that if he had played, we would have won. And when we win, he is still disappointed because if he had played instead of another undeserving fellow, we would have won by an even bigger margin.

After a while, he gets tired of being the twelfth man. He keeps asking to play, only for Bhuvan to deny him. One day, Vendu Murugan has had enough and tells Bhuvan he is just hogging a place in the team and not letting better players play. Bhuvan then organizes a test for Vendu Murugan because it is not safe to play him directly as he has thick glasses.

So Bhuvan and Vendu Murugan land up at my house. Vendu Murugan is told that if he can take ten straight catches, he can play. I am the neutral party to hit catches. I do it straight at Sriram, and not too fast. Bhuvan gets twitchy after five catches and says, 'Hey, hit difficult catches. We can't play him.'

'Why?' I ask.

'He has challenged my authority. Can't you hit a hard catch for a friend?'

So I give him tougher catches, and Vendu Murugan catches the next two as well, one of them a diving catch. Bhuvan wants me to hit harder. I hit the next one really hard; Vendu Murugan gets hit on the hand, and the ball lobs into the next house. He doesn't lose sight of the ball, jumps the wall and catches it in the next house.

Vendu Murugan comes back celebrating, but with a red trail behind him. His webbing has been split, and he is bleeding profusely. Unaware of the blood behind him, he comes back, throws the ball back and gets into the stance for the next catch. 'Two catches left.' With a stitched hand, he shows up for the match the next day and picks up three wickets and the Player-of-the-Match award. He earns a regular place in the RUCA XI and goes on to become an impressive fast bowler, although there is still doubt about whether he properly sights balls that are hit straight back at him.

Venkat. My other best friend. Introduced to RUCA by Santosh and Aravind, his college mates at Hindustan Engineering College.

Excellent at being lazy. Because he is from Trichy and lives alone in Chennai, he spends a lot of time with us. He ends up sleeping over at my place, where he has kept a separate toiletry kit, three-four times a week.

Ashwin. No more just the twelfth-standard player, he is a CSK cricketer now. He is also the coach of the team. We don't have a uniform. Everybody wears an assortment of my jerseys: Tamil Nadu, India Under-19, CSK, Jolly Rovers, Alwarpet. In matches, I always bat towards the end so that everyone can scratch their batting itch.

I am not well-known enough for social weekend teams to recognize me. When I go out to bat, the score is often not much for 6 or 7, and I walk to attacking fields and sledging fielders. Then my competitive juices start flowing, and Vivek and I add big runs.

By now, Appa has installed a 15-yard-long net in our house. This is where most of our fun happens. This is where Vendu Murugan improves so much that he gives me batting practice. This is where I copy Harbhajan Singh and Sunil Narine, bowl legspin, bowl left-arm and bat left-hand. This is where I develop a taste for coaching, which helps me as I help others.

* * *

Our routine with RUCA is to play in the street and then land up at Muthu's soup shop. We shoot the breeze, have the soup and then Venkat, Vivek and I move to Citi Centre shopping mall. We hang out there for a bit, have some sweet corn and then watch a movie at Inox in the mall. Venkat ends up sleeping over half the days.

If he has slept over, in the morning we go together for my cricket. He leaves me there, then goes home, picks up his bike, and then either goes to college or comes back to watch my game.

Venkat is different from all the other RUCA teammates. We are young men and competitive cricketers—there is a bit of an edge. It's not nasty or harmful, but there is a bit of a competitiveness. Venkat has none of that for me. He always looks out for me like a brother.

My RUCA friends are not shy of reminding me of my competitors every time they do well. It is good-spirited banter, but Venkat takes it as a challenge to me and takes the fight to the others in the middle of the street. 'He is no match for Ashwin,' Venkat says. 'What are you even talking about? Have you watched the two of them bowl? There is no comparison. If Ashwin is unwell or unavailable, then the other fellow can play.'

Yet, Venkat is the best at leaving emotions aside in cricket. He wins the most in the fantasy game on krishcricket.com. He doesn't go for his favourite players but those likely to do well even if they are Aussies playing against India. He even won a phone after playing the game.

Venkat's family has taken a hefty loan for his education. He wants to do his bit to ease the load by working while he studies. What he wants to do happens to be his dream: radio jockeying. He eventually wants to be a VJ for Sun TV. I come to know of a talent hunt at Radio Mirchi, a popular radio station.

A few days later, the person who helped us get him in tells me I have got a great friend. I tell him I know, but he says, 'You don't have any idea how good a friend he is.'

I am intrigued. So, my contact tells me, 'There is a round in our audition where competitors are asked to speak about anything they want, but engagingly. Venkat spoke about you for fifteen minutes, saying how you will be the best cricketer to have come out of Tamil Nadu. Either you are going to end up as one of the great cricketers or he is the best friend you can ask for.'

Why can't it be both, I wonder, trusting Venkat's earnestness.

One person who is not earnest is Vivek. He studied with me in PSSB and played decent cricket, but has improved a lot now. He studies at another college, Tagore Engineering College, so he joins us only in the evening.

Vivek is the master of exaggeration. To the extent that when we hear him give an accurate description, we commemorate it by shouting, 'Hey, he is speaking the truth.' He likes to tell tall tales. If you believe him, he knows everybody in the world.

Vivek's father doesn't allow him sleepovers. When Venkat and I are alone, we audit Vivek's exaggerations and have a good laugh. In his presence, though, I tend to let Vivek's embellishments slide.

We have nicknamed him Periyappa after the character played by the actor Visu in the Tamil movie *Pattukottai Periyappa*. Periyappa helps resolve a grave rift between two families through well-meaning lies and deception.

When we are not in Citi Centre mall post Muthu's soups, the three of us can be found at Alwarpet Juice Corner for their chocolate milkshake, which is out of this world. We hang around there also because girls come there.

Venkat is often on the phone because he is in a serious relationship. I keep getting my calls often. When we come back a song plays on Vivek's phone, and he answers the call and starts talking. I know he is pretending but I don't point it out. He makes this a habit.

On one of the nights, we are having a milkshake at Alwarpet Juice Corner, and in the middle of a funny conversation, the same song plays on his phone. The annoyance because of the interruption gets the better of me, and I grab his phone. There are no calls in his call log.

When we ask him what he gains from it, an embarrassed Vivek, says, 'Cheap tricks, *ra*. You guys keep getting calls all the time, so I also need to have something.'

The beauty about Vivek is that he doesn't let anything linger. He drops one charade and moves on to the next one seamlessly.

10

In no time at all, the serious cricket season begins. Again, I am selected for the Challenger Trophy in Nagpur. This year, I am part of India Red, which is led by my Tamil Nadu captain S. Badrinath, and has Ishant Sharma, Ravindra Jadeja, M. Vijay and Shikhar Dhawan.

In the first match, we come up against M.S. Dhoni's India Blue. We win the toss and choose to bat. We get bowled out for 248 but put up an excellent defence. I have been looking forward to bowling to MS in a match situation. I have waited for this for about two years. He is the CSK captain and also the India captain. I have to impress him in a competitive environment. He is both my idol and my captain. I am trying to prove a point in a tight defence.

There is turn in this pitch. Harbhajan Singh took three of our wickets. I feel like I am bowling beautifully. I have nailed MS down, and he can't really score quickly off me. Then I beat him comprehensively through the gate, but the ball bounces just over the top of the stumps. This is extremely disappointing for me. I end up with figures of 10-2-33-1 but not MS's wicket.

Soon MS unleashes a ferocious cut off Ishant, and I am fielding at sweeper-cover. I run in, put in a big dive and catch it to break into wild celebrations as if this is the biggest wicket ever. Abhinav Mukund, my Tamil Nadu teammate but now on MS's side for the

Challenger Trophy, asks me if I really needed that extravagant celebration for MS's catch.

India Blue hang in to win by one wicket, but we come face-to-face again in the final. We bowl them out for 84. Munaf Patel takes four wickets, Sudeep Tyagi three, Ishant two, and I one. My only wicket is that of their top scorer, M.S. Dhoni, caught by Ishant at mid-off. Again, I celebrate big, unable to keep in mind what Abhinav told me. I end up with 27 overs, 84 runs and four wickets, another successful Challenger Trophy.

Post the final, MS doesn't express any displeasure about my celebration. We even add each other as Facebook friends. So I keep in touch with him. We keep having random chats.

The next month, I get my first India call-up for the two T20Is against Sri Lanka in Nagpur and Mohali. The formal confirmation comes through a letter from the BCCI to the TNCA and then to me, but I receive a phone call well before that, when I am on the way from Dharamsala, where we played Himachal Pradesh, to Sambalpur, where we are scheduled to play Orissa. I get a teammate to take my picture, which I make my Orkut display picture. I use the Orkut bio as an MSN status message, which is always updated with the state of mind. Today, I write, 'long way to go', just to remind myself not to be content.

In Dharamsala, I scored a hundred from 132 for 6 and a fifty in the second innings to help us win outright on a fast bowler's track. I finish the game against Orissa. Here I am duck-out, and take only one wicket. Immediately after that, Dinesh Karthik and I travel to Nagpur while the rest of the Tamil Nadu team goes to Mumbai.

My parents are joyful but not surprised. It turns out that V.B. Chandrasekar had already caught wind of it and alerted my cousin that I might be selected, who in turn told my parents. Even before I can tell them that my chances of playing the match in Nagpur are slim, they have already made plans to come and watch me.

I get to Nagpur and am picked up by a hotel car at the airport. Pride Hotel is not too far from the airport. A room has been booked for me, and there is a letter waiting for me at the reception.

It is from the team and has information about the practice timings and when to report for the team bus the next day. I will meet the rest of the team for the first time on the team bus.

Although I have played the Challenger Trophy against and with some of the players, I have not been formally introduced to anyone other than MS and DK. It is possible they don't even remember me. I quietly walk into the bus and start looking for a place tentatively because I have heard big players always sit in the same seat.

I feel it is safest to sit on the last seat, but once I get there, I remember that MS always sits on the last seat in the CSK bus. So, I take the least likely seat to be taken. The last seat has no aisle; it is just one unbroken plank. I take the middle seat. Then MS comes in, I say hello to him and he takes his last window seat.

Just before the bus leaves, MS tells me, 'Don't sit there.'

Wow, what are the odds? This seat is taken too, I think.

I ask MS, 'Does anyone sit here?'

MS replies, 'No, no, anyone who sits here goes out of the Indian team.'

As I don't intend for any such thing to happen, I get up and move to another seat in front. It turns out to be Ishant Sharma's seat. So, I sit somewhere else, and finally we get moving.

I don't have the courage to introduce myself to everyone, and there is no formal way of introducing a new player to the group. I just get there, warm up and start bowling in the nets. There is no Sachin Tendulkar in the T20I squad, but I get to bowl to Virender Sehwag and Gautam Gambhir, both of whom I rate highly as players of spin.

MS's attempt to ward off bad luck doesn't work. I had probably already sat in that cursed seat for long enough. I don't get the opportunity to play in the two T20Is, and Harbhajan Singh is back for the ODI series. Off I go to the Ranji Trophy, but later in the season, I get called up for the home ODI series against South Africa.

I finally meet Sachin. I'm not sure how to address him. I definitely can't call him Sachin, and I don't want to call him 'sir' either. If he knew Tamil, Sachin Anna would have worked. I am relieved when I hear everyone addressing him as 'Paaji'. As far as I know, it is a term used for a big brother in Punjabi. More randomly, it is common to call any Sardar 'paaji', the way it is 'anna' for us. How close I am to realizing the dream of batting with him and the partnerships with him that I visualized as a kid. Except that, in the intervening time, I have become a bowler, and am not getting into the playing XI.

Somehow, I hit the jackpot even when running drinks. In the second ODI, in Gwalior, Sachin is hitting everyone all over the ground. As the innings goes on, I start thinking of the elusive double-century that no man has scored in ODI cricket. Sachin has come close twice, but it has somehow eluded him. It is a humid evening, so towards the end, I have to run out almost every over.

Inside the dressing room, Virender Sehwag, or 'Viru Pa' as M. Vijay addresses him, and now I do too, is not moving from his seat. Yuvraj Singh is Yuvi Pa, and Harbhajan Singh is Bhajju Pa. Not moving from your seat is the most common superstition in dressing rooms. There is so much in cricket that is out of control. It is not unusual for cricketers, especially batters, to try to control through superstition or routines what can't be controlled otherwise. Viru Pa doesn't want to jinx Paaji. He is not even cheering for Paaji's shots.

Carrying drinks for Paaji is not a mundane, mechanical job. On one occasion, he tells me, 'Ask Kaka to be ready.' Kaka is Ramesh Mane, the genial masseur of the Indian cricket team. Kaka means 'uncle' in Marathi. There couldn't be a more apt way to address Mane Kaka. Apart from being an ace masseur, he is a good-vibes man. He plays devotional songs in the dressing room, and I am told he cooks Indian food and makes Indian spiced milky tea for the boys when those things are not readily available on international tours.

Paaji doesn't want to waste any time. As soon as the innings ends, he will go straight to Kaka for treatment so that he can be back on the field in the second innings.

On another occasion, as I am pouring him water, Paaji asks, 'Do I look very tired when I am running?'

I say no. He tells me it is very draining and to keep water ready.

Every time I go back, I pinch myself. I am talking to Sachin Tendulkar. In the flesh. Here is this batting genius playing a dream innings but also wanting to glean every bit of information possible to check if he has slowed down or anything like that.

Towards the end of the innings, MS starts to take too much of the strike, but Paaji gets just enough balls to get to the first-ever double-hundred in men's ODI cricket. We go on to win the match easily and seal the series. Again, I don't get to play in a match.

I go back to the Ranji Trophy one-dayers after the series, just in time for the final in Ahmedabad. DK scores a beautiful 88 off 47 balls to turn what looks like a 320 into a 379. It turns out we need each one of those extra runs as Bengal get to 350. I don't get a wicket, but I and L. Balaji are the only bowlers in our side to go at under six an over. Despite opening the bowling and operating in the powerplay, which has become my specialty.

Another trophy for Tamil Nadu. A title successfully defended.

* * *

S. Badrinath, my Tamil Nadu captain and CSK teammate, and I have a theory about horses and captains. Each captain is different. Some can make donkeys run. Some people can buy wounded horses, treat them, train them, and make them run. But M.S. Dhoni will only make a racehorse run. He needs to be convinced you're a racehorse before he makes you run. He will wait for a racehorse. If he doesn't believe you're a racehorse, he'll probably give you the time to become one, but he won't make you run if you aren't there yet.

And I believe MS has seen enough of me in the nets and the Challenger Trophy to notice the racehorse in me. He will make me run for CSK in the 2010 IPL. Stephen Fleming has retired and stepped into the coaching role last year, but this year, he is looking forward to the season with excitement. He desperately wants CSK to be champions, so he is looking at every small advantage we can take.

Flem's one big change for the season is wanting all eleven players on the field to have a play on the ball when it is hit. Basically, don't move only when you think you are in play. Move first, and then get eliminated if you're not going to be in play. For example, if a ball is hit towards deep cover, the fielder running for it should have a backup running with him. Mid-off should move to the bowler's end to collect the throw. There should be backup for both ends to prevent overthrows. Even fine leg and mid-on should be alert in case there is a ricochet off a direct hit. So all eleven fielders have to move for 120 balls when we are in the field. I have never seen a coach plan this minutely.

MS doesn't speak much during meetings. He listens to different points of view and just absorbs them. He accepts everyone's ideas. He also allows people to emote. Then he reflects on them before responding. He never reacts in a hurry. He doesn't interrupt Flem's job of preparing the players. He hardly attends the bowlers' meetings.

On most occasions, we turn up at the ground, and Flem announces the XI plus a twelfth man. This is when things get visibly serious. The rest of the players and the rest of the support staff leave. Only the twelve and Flem remain in the room. Even here, MS allows everyone to say their piece. Everyone talks briefly about what their plan for the game is. MS just listens, and when it is his turn to speak, he says, 'All good, let's go.'

It is at the last possible moment, in the huddle outside, that MS takes charge. Now, he is switched on. He talks about what we are going to do in the powerplay, which bowlers should remain mentally prepared to bowl inside the powerplay, where he wants the fielders positioned, who will save the singles and who will sit back on the 30-yard circle. If we have batted already, he tells us how the pitch is behaving. This, out on the field, is his only team meeting where MS speaks.

Sometimes, if the opposition has got off to a great start, he calls us together at the end of the powerplay and tells us that the game only begins now. 'Don't worry, we will win.' Then he takes control of the game once the field is spread out.

We don't get off to a great start. Defending champions Deccan Chargers score 190 in the first game. I am the only bowler with a wicket, that of Adam Gilchrist, conceding just 26 in four overs in my first IPL match in India. Once we lose early wickets, we fail to get back into the match. I am duck-out first ball.

After the match, I get a text message: 'Well done, offspinner.' I don't have the number saved but I know it is C.K. Vijayakumar, my coach from St Bede's because I remember his number by heart. I thank him, and his response is: 'I told you that you will play for India as an offspinner. I will message you then too.'

We come back immediately thanks to MS's 66 off 33 against the Kolkata Knight Riders in Kolkata. Albie Morkel and Muthiah Muralidaran give a great start to our defence of 164, and I contribute with figures of 4-0-22-1.

After the game, I witness in person the legend of C. Ganapathy. Ganpa is a popular player in the Tamil Nadu dressing room. And this is not the Punjabi 'pa' at the end. During the crisis after the exodus of players to the ICL, Ganpa rose to the occasion. He is a fast bowler but has also scored two first-class double-centuries. He was also my roommate in first-class cricket.

None of this makes him a legend, though. He is a boisterous, humorous person but not in a subtle way, a bit like the slapstick comedians in Tamil movies. If he has made it to CSK, he will make use of all the facilities: the swimming pool, massages and physiotherapy. Sometimes, he can be unwittingly funny.

I am in the treatment room with Tommy Simsek, our physiotherapist from Australia. He used to be the Sri Lanka physiotherapist, famous for sprinting onto the field whenever a player needed treatment. He likes the boys from Chennai because we don't use him frivolously. He has just given me some treatment for a strain and is looking at KB Arun Karthik. Ganpa comes in and, in a hushed tone, tells Tommy something about his ankle.

Tommy tells him, loudly, 'No worries, mate. Just jump on the bench. I will check it out.'

Tommy goes back to look at KB, and when he turns around, he sees Ganpa has taken two steps back and is ready to pounce.

'May I?' Ganpa asks.

'May I what?' Tommy asks.

'Jump on the bench, Tommy. I thought you wanted to test my ankle by seeing if I could jump.'

Tommy holds his head in his hand and asks him to just get on the bench normally. Before Ganpa is out, KB and I have already narrated this incident to Anirudha Srikkanth. And, as the Tamil Nadu analyst Laxmi Narayanan knows for sure, Ani is the worst person to tell such things to. The story receives many embellishments and becomes a legend in Tamil Nadu cricket circles.

In fact, the person who needs physiotherapy the most is MS, who is hit on the arm when facing Shane Bond. He has been out for a few games now. Suresh Raina is the captain in his absence. In the next game, I open the bowling and go for 1 for 40 in my four overs. Haydos's genius wins us this match against Delhi Daredevils.

In the next match, against Kings XI Punjab, we are coasting towards our target of 137. We are 96 for 1 in the 13th over when Raina is run out. M. Vijay, pushed down the order because MS's replacement, Parthiv Patel, can be best utilized in the powerplay, falls immediately. Panic sets in. Before we know it, I am in with 10 required off eight balls. In front of a home crowd.

Albie Morkel and I hustle, and somehow, we need just one off the last two. The problem is, I am on strike. I miss the fifth ball, and Kumar Sangakkara is smartly standing only a couple of steps back to deny us the bye. Irfan Pathan runs in for the last ball. I see that it is right in my slot. I hit hard, but guess what? It goes straight to Mohammad Kaif at mid-off for a catch. We go on to lose the one-over tiebreaker called the Super Over.

The wheels properly come off in Bangalore, where we play our next match. Raina bowls me in the 13th, 15th, 18th and 20th overs. After a good start, I go for 17 in the last over to make it 40 in four overs. Robin Uthappa is in red-hot form. He reverse sweeps Murali; I run back towards deep cover and somehow, I get my hands on it, but it wobbles out of my hand. Robin has just nearly hit a six left-handed off Murali, and I have dropped the catch.

We lose again, and I am sent back from Bangalore while the rest of the team continues on the road. I've been given no reason for being sent back, nor any instructions on what I need to do better. Two days later, I am asked to go to Ahmedabad for the next game against the Rajasthan Royals. I am expecting to play, but my name doesn't feature in the final twelve, and I go out of the dressing room with the other extras as it is done in CSK.

We go on to lose. The atmosphere on the bus ride to the hotel is tense. Everyone is quiet. Our tournament is almost over. We need to win almost every game now to progress. MS is quiet as usual in the last seat. I am in the aisle seat just a few rows ahead, and Ani is in the next aisle seat. We're grumbling about not getting any opportunities to play.

Amidst all this, suddenly Ganpa, sitting in the window seat next to me, says, 'Ash, party?'

Ganpa and I went to the nightclub called Dublin in Chennai after the first game, and with something or other coming up after that, we haven't had the time to catch up. In any case, CSK are not big on partying, and now is definitely not the time to go partying.

I shush him quietly. He says, 'What? We will go and party.'

Now, Ahmedabad is admittedly not the place to go partying for just the second time in the season, or possibly ever, but there are IPL parties that are exempt from the prohibition rules of the state of Gujarat. Still, this is not a good idea. Not on this night.

MS is right there, but Ganpa is beatboxing and headnodding. Ani jumps in, thankfully using Tamil, but a crass version of it: 'Ganpa, we have lost five games out of seven. We have been disqualified. We are out of the tournament. What party? They will send us home.'

Ganpa is in no mood to relent: 'Hey, what da? This is what I hate. We are professional cricketers. Play while you play. Party while you party. Haven't you heard of that? Game is over, now we go partay. Tomorrow, we practise and get ready for the next match. Then we partay. Partay. Next match. Partay. Next match. Partay. Next match.'

We can't laugh, we can't keep a straight face, and there is this whole situation with the team. I tell him Flem has put a curfew in place. We are not allowed to go.

'What allow?' Ganpa snaps back. 'We are adults. We are all past eighteen. India is a democratic country. What curfew? I will talk to him.'

More beatboxing as he tries to walk towards our security manager. Then Ani shouts, 'Curfew is not a person, Ganpa. It means we have to be back by a certain time.'

And we actually break into laughter. Everyone gives us dirty looks.

I don't need to go to a party to be sent home. Without telling me anything, I am left out of the squad again. Back for one match, not even in the XI, and now back home. I am particularly disappointed in Flem because I really respect him as a coach and expect him to personally tell me I am being dropped. He speaks well with every player, respects everyone, and is a smart coach. But even he hasn't bothered speaking to me.

Is it possible MS doesn't even think I am a racehorse yet?

* * *

Over the next couple of days, I keep wondering what I've done wrong. Yes, I didn't finish the game off with the bat, but nobody has spoken about that to me. In the Bangalore game, I bowled the toughest overs for a spinner. Eventually, when I can't take these thoughts anymore, I call up V.B. Chandrasekar, the selector when I got my first Tamil Nadu call-up and now the director of cricket at CSK.

I ask him why I am being removed from the squad. 'What wrong did I do? What must I do to get back?' VB clearly doesn't like it and tells me they know what they are doing. It's about what they want to do, and they are clear about what they are going to do. He goes on to tell me that I should know that the decision-makers are there because of what they know about the game. I am not satisfied with that, and I keep prodding him. The conversation doesn't end well.

VB, though, has always been a well-wisher. He has always told MS of my ability. He knows my parents. He has always relayed news of my selection through my cousin, who is a good friend of his. This time, his call to my cousin is not a pleasant one. The gist of his communication is: What does your cousin think of himself?

My cousin calls up my parents and tells them that VB is not happy with Ashwin. My parents get extremely worried and ask me what I've done. They even ask me if that is the reason I have been dropped. I tell them this chat happened after the drop. In fact, it happened because of the drop.

Appa scolds me and asks me to be humble. I don't understand what humility has to do with it. I had direct and honest communication with VB, but he didn't reciprocate. Appa tells me VB has always wanted the best for me. I tell him I didn't say anything disrespectful to VB sir. Appa tells me he doesn't have to explain everything to me.

I walk out in a huff because I'd much rather play with my RUCA friends than have an argument where nobody wants to see my point. We are playing in the middle of the street when the young man returning from the hospital hangs around to make sure I am the same guy who failed to score 1 run off 2 balls at Chepauk against Kings XI Punjab.

A good couple of minutes later, he asks me, 'You are the guy who plays for CSK?'

I say yes. And he takes off: 'Sir, it is just one run. Just drop and run, no? Just like you are blocking and running here. Can't you just do that in a game? What's wrong with you?'

It is a terrible moment. Possibly the most humiliated I have ever felt. But I can't say anything to the man. I should have finished the match. We just move our game to the net indoors.

While I am out of the team, I start hearing whispers: 'Who plays such a cricketer in the IPL?' 'He is at best a club cricketer.' There is even an article in a newspaper suggesting I be dropped from the Tamil Nadu Ranji team.

My career may as well be over. Amma sees me despondent and tells me, 'See, last year, you made ten lakh. This year, you made twenty. We will save some more. You are already an engineer. You will get a job. We will also work for ten more years. So what if cricket is not there? You enjoy your life.'

I tell her I know nothing about engineering.

'Which engineer knows anything about engineering?' Amma tries to humour me.

I tell her not to worry because I think MS trusts me. All the more reason for her to say, 'Then you have even less cause for sadness. Just make sure you don't let MS down.'

In a gloomy week where CSK are on a proper losing streak, I get to hear one piece of good news: Abhinav Mukund, my friend from Tamil Nadu, is likely to play the next game in Chennai. So, after the team comes back home, now having won just two games out of seven, I ask the management for a ticket for the match that Abhinav will be playing. I get a call back from the same member of the support staff who wanted me to turn up for the optional training sessions in South Africa. He calls me to the ITC Park Sheraton, where the team is staying.

When I get there, he is in the lobby and hands me an envelope. I open it to find it is a ticket for the A Stand. I am a CSK player, and he is giving me a ticket for a stand with a side view of the action. When I used to go with Appa, I would make sure to buy Pavilion Terrace tickets even when they were beyond our means.

When I ask for a better ticket, one with a straight view, I am not prepared for the outburst that follows. I am told I am too small a player to be making such high demands or asking so many questions. That I should be happy with what is being given to me.

I become conscious of people looking at us. I speak in a low tone so as not to draw more attention. 'I'm not questioning you, sir, I just want to know if it's possible to get a better ticket,' I say, adding, 'I am asking for a straight view so that I can enjoy the game as well as learn something.'

He flies off the handle, telling me I am completely out of my depth as a cricketer. I can't even focus on the exact words. The embarrassment of people stopping what they are doing and looking at us is too much to handle. I leave the envelope at the reception desk, tell him I don't need his ticket and walk off. I feel so little that someone not in charge of the cricketing side of operations is also taking a dump on me.

The next day, Kasi Viswanathan, the right-hand man of N. Srinivasan and the CEO of CSK, calls me. He is nice and respectful, the complete opposite of what I had encountered yesterday. He says he heard I had an issue with the tickets offered to me. He says, 'We don't have better tickets, da. We have already given the Pavilion Terrace tickets to someone else. There are only A Stand tickets left. Now take it and go watch the game. For the next game, we will arrange better ones.'

I tell him I could have been told that yesterday instead of being humiliated. I politely decline the A Stand ticket, tell him I will take him up on his promise in the next match and instead watch the match on TV with my RUCA friends. Abhi doesn't get to play, but Ganpa does. He is brought on in the 10th over. He starts off well but bowls two full tosses in the second half of the over. MS doesn't bowl him after that. Ganpa is my friend, but I am thinking to myself why I don't get the luxury of starting in the 10th over.

Ganpa is in the middle on duck not out when we finish the win, thanks to M. Vijay's 78 off 39 balls, but I am not there to party with him. Kasi, though, doesn't have to keep the promise of arranging better tickets for the next match because I will not be needing any tickets.

* * *

I receive a call asking me to report to the team hotel and re-join the squad. I tell him I would have preferred Flem calling me. 'He should just speak to me and, you know, tell me what they expect from me. It's not you who should be calling,' I say.

Anyway, I proceed to checking into my room. Soon, Flem calls me and asks to meet. He tells me I am back in the mix and that the team is looking forward to having me back. 'It is possible Suresh didn't use you properly, but now MS is back,' he says. 'MS will utilize you well.'

I tell Flem how disappointed I was that he didn't speak to me when I was sent home. I tell him how much I value his opinion and how I expected him to call me later, if not at that moment.

Flem tells me I am right, but he also tells me he got caught up in the whirlwind of running the team when the full-time captain is missing and the team is losing. He tells me he can see how hard it must have been for me. I see sense in what he says, and I now look forward to being back. Those jobs as an engineer who knows nothing about engineering can wait.

I am not back immediately, but in the next game against the Rajasthan Royals, I witness two special events. Vijay plays an absolutely breathtaking innings against an attack of Shane Warne, Shane Watson and Shaun Tait. He plays some audacious shots but with a silken touch, scoring 127 off just 56 balls to take us to 246.

In the dugout, I am sitting next to Murali. It is quite an obvious thing to do: he is an offspinner, and we both speak Tamil. I try to learn as much as I can from him. I tell him how Vijay's innings could be just the motivation we need to turn the season around. He is like a nervous child, hoping for more runs even when we have crossed 220. He is just cheering the batters on and asking for more runs to defend.

I tell him, 'You are Muralidaran, man. You have the big offbreak, you have the *doosra*, and you have so much experience. With you, we should win even with 170.'

'But Naman Ojha will slog-sweep, no?' Murali says.

I am amazed that even Murali has self-doubt. I am immediately reminded of the conversations when Kepler Wessels was the coach. Murali would hardly ever go at over a run a ball, but he was not getting many wickets because teams used to choose to play him out and attack the others. Wessels would tell him he is the best bowler in the world; he needs to pick up more wickets. Instead of retaliating, Murali would take it on board. There are these inhuman expectations of him, but he doubts himself too, just like other humans.

Ojha, by the way, scores an unbeaten 94 and takes the Rajasthan Royals close even though we win fairly comfortably. Murali, though, gives him just 11 off the 10 balls he bowls to him.

I am in the XI for the next match against the Mumbai Indians. We are defending 165, and MS throws the ball to me in the fourth over. Perhaps he senses something. He tells me, 'I know it's Sachin Paaji, but you are as good as him.'

I am still trying to figure out the situation. After all, this is Sachin Tendulkar I am bowling to. From bowling to him in the nets, I know that Paaji hardly ever comes forward to spin, and when he does, he does so to attack. I think what he does is try to make the bowler feel like he is too short. Even if you bowl full and he goes back, he has a little extra time because of his height. When he successfully makes you bowl too full, he is lethal against it.

That's what Paaji does to me in my first two overs. First, he goes back to cut a decently full ball for four. Then, when I overpitch, he launches me over mid-on. Here we go again. I have already conceded 16 off my first two overs; when I am brought back, there will probably be Kieron Pollard to contend with.

Luckily, we pick wickets when I am out of the attack, and they are already four down by the time I come back. Then I bowl to Pollard, and he mis-hits a big shot for a really high catch. It has gone so high that Thilan Thushara, too, gets close to the ball, even though it is Vijay's catch. At the last moment, Thushara comes in front of Vijay and drops the catch. However, Vijay just sticks his hand out in desperation, and the ball sticks. I believe now that luck is changing.

In the next match, our batting fails, and despite my figures of 4-0-13-2 we lose, which means we can't afford slip-ups if we are to stay alive in the tournament.

Against the Kolkata Knight Riders in Chennai, we lose the toss, and MS gives me the brand-new ball because KKR have two left-hand openers: Chris Gayle and Sourav Ganguly. MS tells me, 'Both of them can hit; they both play spin well; just make sure you keep it flat for Dada.'

Dada is Sourav Ganguly. Just like *paaji* and *pa*, *dada* is Bengali for big brother. And MS is right: Dada is lethal when he steps out. So he wants me to keep it flat to keep Dada in his crease. I bowl a good first over, conceding just three singles.

I start the second over to Gayle. He steps out and mis-hits the ball. Dropped from the squad, brought back, and about to repay MS's trust in me with the huge wicket of Gayle, I look back to see who is going to catch it. Nobody. Because this mis-hit has comfortably cleared the boundary and landed on top of the Madras Cricket Club roof.

MS runs up to me and says, 'Give a single to him. Just get him off strike.'

I turn around to go to my mark, and I am thinking, 'This is the moment I've always wanted. Chris Gayle is in front of me; he has hit me for a six. I've bowled a good ball, and he has tonked me. What is my best option now? I have to bowl at his pads just to be quick. Can I get a yorker in?'

I am immediately reminded of Bangalore, where Robin Uthappa and Mark Boucher hit my yorkers for sixes. So I tell myself to just spin the ball up and slow it down. I do that, and Gayle is out of the crease again, but the ball drops on him, and he walks past it as it turns. MS breaks the wicket in a flash and charges at me, pumping his fists. 'I didn't expect you to slow it up, man,' he says. 'Amazing. Just amazing.'

MS just walks around pumping his fists, hitting his left hand with his right fist. I've never seen MS so elated and so animated. He is reacting like a man who has found his racehorse.

When Brendon McCullum comes out, I tell MS that I want to bowl the carrom ball to him. MS tells me to do that. 'What field do you want?' I say we don't need to change the field, and I still want long-on and midwicket back. MS asks me, 'Why not long-off back?' I tell him not to worry and that I will bowl straight lines, and that the long-off back will telegraph the move too.

I don't bowl the carrom ball immediately. I slip it in one ball later, and McCullum is trapped right in front, but the umpire, Simon Taufel, doesn't give it out probably because he has never seen a carrom ball before. I get McCullum two balls later off the top edge on a sweep. That's the end of my second over. My figures in a must-win match: 2-0-9-2.

At the start of the next over, I get nice dip on a straight offbreak to David Hussey, who falls over trying to defend it, is beaten, and MS stumps him like lightning. This is the best stumping I have ever seen as it is not easy to sight the ball down the leg side as it comes across the batter. This is called a wide, but I am on a hat-trick now.

MS gives me all the close-in fielders for the hat-trick ball. Angelo Mathews defends in front of the body; the ball turns in, takes his glove, and goes straight to leg slip. I can't believe I have a hat-trick. We are all celebrating, but Umpire Taufel rules it not-out. Never mind. I still go on to be the Player of the Match as we win easily and boost our net run rate too by finishing off the chase in the 14th over.

Remarkably, we are still alive in the competition after having thought it was all over on that Ahmedabad bus ride, but our hopes still hang by a thread. A thread that gets even weaker when we lose to Delhi Daredevils at home. On a turning track, we put up a spirited defence of just 112, but two of the best players of spin in India, Gautam Gambhir and Mithun Manhas, see DD home.

Since we've won our matches by a big margin, and thanks to some other results, we still have our fate in our hands when we go to Dharamsala to play Kings XI Punjab. If we lose, we finish sixth, but our net run rate is so good that even if we win by the slenderest of margins, we will finish third on the table.

I bowl four overs for 20 and take Kumar Sangakkara's wicket in their innings of 192. We are struggling in the chase, but Badri and Raina keep us alive. We need 16 off the last over. Irfan Pathan bowls a pretty good yorker, but MS goes deep in the crease to hit it wide of long-off for four. Our dugout is right behind the long-off fielder. We can see how ferocious the hit is.

Irfan bowls a slower ball next; MS mis-hits, but it falls short of long-off. Piyush Chawla misfields right in front of us, and MS marches off for the second. Two near-perfect balls and still six runs conceded, and MS is not even off the strike. Then Irfan errs, as bowlers do because they are not machines. It is just short of being a yorker, and MS unleashes a monster hit over wide long-on. The dugout is going crazy; even Flem is on his feet and cheering.

The next ball meets the same fate, and MS emotes like I have never seen him emote before. That reaction to the Gayle wicket was nothing. He exults and then punches himself in the helmet grille. Murali, who has been left out, also rushes out of the dugout like an eighteen-year-old, his bib split open from the front. Our guys nearly run Piyush over as they all rush to MS to celebrate. Later, MS says it is an emotional moment for him because the franchise deserves at least a semi-final qualification, not at the last moment like this.

This was a special feeling. MS was under a lot of pressure as he hadn't scored big runs in the first two years. Raina was struggling. Haydos, who carried us last year, was struggling. In the middle of the season, we were wondering where the inspiration would come from. Then Vijay provided the spark, and Dougie Bollinger, MS and I came through.

Dougie breaks open the semi-final with a sensational opening spell, and when I get Andrew Symonds later, I break into a big celebration. He is a big wicket, and their last recognized batter. We are into the final now against the best team of the league stage, the Mumbai Indians, at their home ground, D.Y. Patil Stadium in Navi Mumbai, a place that Appa and I never explored when we would go to Bombay to watch Test matches.

Before the final, I overhear a couple of players talking, 'Does he even know who Symonds is? Tell him to be careful. He will smash him.' I assume they are talking about my big celebration after getting Symonds out in the semi-final.

On the day of the final, the 12 for the match are presented with a special jersey. In defence of 168, I take the new ball as I have been doing and bowl a maiden over to Shikhar Dhawan. Bollinger gets him in the next over. It turns out that MI are backloading as they promote Abhishek Nayar and Harbhajan Singh. It's great if they come off; not much is lost if they don't. But they get the worst outcome. We give them nothing, and neither Nayar nor Sachin Paaji, playing with a split webbing, gets away with any big hits. By the time Ambati Rayudu and Kieron Pollard get in, their ask is massive.

Pollard gives them hope with 22 runs off Dougie in the 18th over, but we are still confident with 33 needed in two overs. Still, to be sure, MS introduces a field he has discussed with us before, but in general and not specifically for Pollard. He has a straight mid-off and a long-off right behind him. They are so straight that they are almost on the sight screen. With us, MS had only mentioned in passing that this is a field one can work with; there was no elaborate planning. And out it comes, with the final on the line.

Albie Morkel now bowls only yorkers knowing Pollard likes to hit them straight, so MS is probably happy to sacrifice one fielder elsewhere. It works, as Pollard is caught low at mid-off by Haydos. MS's celebration for the remarkable plan is unremarkable.

Six balls later, we are the IPL champions after believing we were out nine games ago. We have won seven of these nine games. Ganpa still doesn't get the opportunity to party hard. CSK is not that kind of team. Besides, there are five days between the IPL final and India's first match of the T20 World Cup in the West Indies. There is no time to party. My second wind in this IPL comes too late to take me to the World Cup because the ICC requires squads to be submitted a month in advance.

MS, Flem and Suresh tell me I have done a big job for them by bowling with the new ball. Amma, I haven't let MS down.

11

While the Indian team goes to the West Indies for the T20 World Cup, I come back to West Mambalam to play with my friends from RUCA. We play cricket at 4 p.m. and then while away our time. The usual places for our sessions are the ramp outside our house, the boundary wall of any house or the stools around Muthu's soup stall.

One day, we are just sitting and having soup and generally making a nuisance of ourselves when an elderly man approaches us. In a deep, booming voice, almost a baritone, he says, 'Ashwin sir, how are you?'

He is at least sixty years old, if I'm not mistaken. As he grabs one of the stools, I realize he has no interest in knowing how I am. The RUCA boys make sure he sits close to me so that they can't be seen when they are giggling behind his back.

Our man continues in his baritone: 'Sir, that over to Chris Gayle was sooper, sir. Like this only, I used to watch Yerapalli Prasanna bowl, sir. Yerapalli Prasanna also used to toss the ball. It would be on a string, sir.'

I struggle to keep a straight face while the boys giggle behind him. For twenty minutes, he regales us with his stories of watching 'Yerapalli' Prasanna, Venkataraghavan and Bishan Singh Bedi. B.S. Chandrasekhar doesn't get proportionate mentions.

When leaving, he asks, 'Have you . . . have you, gone to Venkat sir? Go to him for tips. He is a fantastic bowler.'

I politely reply, saying I don't know how to approach him. And he immediately says, 'Sir, my relative is a friend of Venkataraghavan. Give me your number, and I will send his number to you.'

I am dumbfounded because I don't know how to tell him I can't give him my number. Vicky comes to my rescue and tells him, 'Sir, he doesn't remember his number. Let me give it to you.' And he proceeds to give him his own number.

Vicky saves his number under the name 'Military Uncle' because of his booming voice.

* * *

By the time I make my debut for India, with most of the seniors resting for the Zimbabwe tour, I've been with the team so often that it doesn't feel special. In fact, I now begin to feel a little disappointed whenever I have to leave the Tamil Nadu team dressing room. We have a good all-round side: we are winning, we enjoy playing with each other, and the India call-up just results in me sitting on the bench. When I'm away, I miss my friends, my colleagues and all the fun we have, so I enjoy returning to the Tamil Nadu dressing room.

This Zimbabwe tour, though, is in June, which is Tamil Nadu's off season. I am expecting to make my debut in the Bulawayo leg of games, but I finally play in Harare against Sri Lanka. We lose and don't make it to the final of the tri-series, but I take the wickets of the centurion Dinesh Chandimal and Upul Tharanga. It is perhaps enough for the selectors to keep me in the squad when the senior players return for the Asia Cup in Sri Lanka.

My favourite number is 9, because that was my roll number in school. In 2008, when CSK asked me which number I wanted on my jersey, I asked for 9, but Parthiv Patel already had the number. So I went for 99. When I got called up to the Indian side, Amit Mishra already had 99, so I went back to 9. That is the jersey number I carry to Sri Lanka.

Viru Pa is ruled out with a hamstring injury just before the final. That gives DK a chance to resume his stop-and-start international career. I want to send my positive vibes and energy to DK so I insist that he play the final in my jersey, and he agrees. He sticks masking tape over my name and goes out to open in my No. 9 jersey, which is a little too loose for him. He ends up scoring a fifty and taking the Player-of-the-Match award as we beat Sri Lanka by eighty-one runs.

A couple of months later, I find myself in Sri Lanka again for a tri-series against New Zealand and Sri Lanka. There is a big party on the day I land because the Test side has chased down 258 at P. Sara Oval to end the series 1-1. V.V.S. Laxman has scored an unbeaten 103 despite an injury. Because Suresh Raina is batting with Laxman, Viru Pa is the by-runner for Laxman. Chasing and winning in Sri Lanka is not easy, so they are celebrating the win before we move to Dambulla for the ODIs.

I go into the party and quickly step out. I still feel out of place. These are big players. I know I am not someone they will recognize when they are partying after such a big win. In my case, acceptance will come only with performance because, aesthetically, nothing stands out about me when I bowl in the nets. No one watches me bowl and goes, 'Wow.'

I genuinely need that acceptance, though, to lose that feeling of being in awe all the time. I want to be one of them as soon as possible. So I'm always trying to analyse how they are looking at me. What is running through their heads? Do they think I am a proper cricketer or just a guy to make up the numbers? Do they think I am going to have a long India career or just be an IPL wonder? Do they know of my other performances or do they think I am an IPL product?

Unfortunately, there is a lot of time to think about all that because I'm not getting a game anytime soon. However, there is some semblance of an answer on this trip. Gary Kirsten, the coach of the team, has a chat with me before the start of the series.

'Look, you could genuinely play the World Cup,' Gary tells me. 'There are areas in this team where you can complement us.

You could really be that bowler, that enforcer or the X factor that we are looking at. And you can also bat and contribute in the field. So, we want you to work on these areas.'

'Just do a little bit more fielding than you're used to. You may have to stand in the deep, at long-on or deep midwicket because we have a team in which there are a lot of senior players. You're not one of the quickest, but we believe you've got really good hands, and we can work on your fielding to get you better. So, can you really contribute and field every day?

'For now, we would definitely like you to run along with Paddy every day.'

Paddy is Paddy Upton. On paper, Paddy is India's mental conditioning coach, but he is much more than that. He knows a lot about physical training as well. More importantly, he is Gary's sounding board, his eyes and ears. He feeds Gary things such as what the team likes, how he should approach certain situations and how he should address losses. They work really well as a team.

MS has a completely different operational style. He isn't overwhelmed by wins and losses. When we lose, we come back like it's business as usual. No one says anything. I think to myself, 'This is a bit weird. So, that's it? We've lost, and no one's going to say anything? Aren't there going to be any changes?' I wonder how this team can be so chilled out.

The World Cup, to be played in India next year, is still six months away, and I have barely played any international cricket. So I'm under no illusions about being able to play in the World Cup. I think that perhaps Gary and Paddy want the next generation to be more fitness-friendly. That they want us youngsters to upscale ourselves. The World Cup carrot is just some extra motivation.

As a player on the bench, I want to improve every day. I don't want people telling me that I'm unfit. I don't want people to say I'm lazy. I want to be ready. I don't want to be in a situation in which I'm found lacking what it takes. This is the first time the team management has told me they will help me get there.

Once the toss has happened, Paddy takes me on five to six laps of the ground in the hot and muggy conditions. Sometimes our trainer, Ramji Srinivasan, monitors the fitness activity. Dambulla is an open ground with hardly any crowd, so it is easier to train in the main ground even on match days. Gary and Paddy make sure I am running into the wind, and the wind is stiff in Dambulla. In the innings break, they make me field for half an hour.

I have loved running since childhood. I believe the more I run, the fitter I get. Saurabh Tiwary, from the same state as MS, is often my running partner. When we come back exhausted, Saurabh goes, 'Coconut water, 10.' I drink two or three of those. And then: 'Sandwiches, 12.' Saurabh doesn't know single digits. In the background, there is always Rohit Sharma pulling Pragyan Ojha's leg.

These are fun times. I enjoy bowling in the nets much more, not that it wasn't enjoyable earlier. I bowl to great players of spin who are vastly different from each other. You can bowl a straight line to MS and sometimes get him when he's defending. Sachin Paaji might defend that same ball or slog-sweep it. You bowl that same delivery to Viru Pa, and he will move aside and cut.

It is competitive, at least for me. If Viru Pa has smashed me, I go back and think about what I should do to him the next day. It's not even a match, but that's how I approach the nets sessions. I try to figure out his weaknesses. Does he sweep? He doesn't sweep. Can I go around the wicket? Can I go outside leg stump to him as an offspinner. Most people say that's a defensive line, but for Viru Pa, it could be an attacking line.

He has smashed Murali all his life. There has to be a reason. W.V. Raman used to tell me that the easiest way to play spin is to hit against the spin. If you get beside the line and hit it against the spin, there are fewer fielders on that side. As there are a lot of revs on the ball, you just need to time it for it to fly off. Raman used to talk about how Mohammad Azharuddin had that philosophy and what a good player of spin he was. Some geniuses see things like this differently. So, I try to take away Viru Pa's shots against the spin.

Then there is Gautam Gambhir. He can cut the same ball fine of short third, and also step out and hit it over cover. You can't expect to bowl the same ball and expect the same response from him all the time. It seems impossible for a spinner to tie him down in white-ball cricket. If you want to bowl in the same area, you need to change your speed. You need to change the revs on the ball and the angle on the ball for him to defend the ball. If he defends the ball, you can congratulate yourself: you have just beaten him in flight.

I love the challenge of bowling to Gautam not only because he dominates spinners but also because, as a captain, he rates them. The nets behind the main ground in Dambulla have good pitches with bounce and a little bit of turn. I get his edge every now and then. I also manage to make him work hard for his big shots.

Now, I'm being acknowledged by batters whenever I bowl a good ball at them. After almost every session, Gautam gives me feedback. He appreciates me during the session every time I make him defend. 'I think you should play,' he often tells me. 'You'll get your chances. Just hang in there.'

On the way back from training sessions, Paddy asks for the bus to stop around 5–6 km before the resort we are staying in. Six to seven of us jump off, and then we all run through the forest trail all the way to the resort so that Saurabh is exhausted and ready to order food in double digits.

* * *

The Champions League T20 and I have not had a great relationship so far. When it was first scheduled in 2008, I was named in the squad, but the terror attack in Mumbai resulted in the cancellation of the tournament. In 2009, we didn't make the IPL final, so we didn't even qualify. In 2010, though, we are IPL champions, and I am going to play. This is the first overseas tour in which I know I will get a good run in the starting XI.

We start off with an easy win against New Zealand's Central Districts. Murali and I take two wickets apiece. We run through Wayamba from Sri Lanka next. Ajantha Mendis goes for 45 runs in his four overs, and I pick up four wickets. We are both known for our carrom balls, but in this tournament, I am using my topspinner more because of the bounce available in South Africa.

We move to Port Elizabeth next, where we face Victoria from Australia. I stop the marauding Aaron Finch with a carrom ball that he edges back to me. He scores 41 off 17, which makes the job of others in the chase of 163 easier. Suresh Raina and Dougie Bollinger bowl us to a tiebreaker when all is lost.

While we are getting ready for the Super Over tiebreaker, I see that MS has not yet made a clear decision. Or at least that's what I think. As we are coming back together, I raise my hand and say, 'I'd like to bowl the over if you are okay with that.'

MS says, 'All good, let's go.' I start with a quick full delivery, nearly a yorker, and Finch takes a single off a bottom edge. David Hussey is his partner. I bowl what I feel is a decent offbreak second ball, but he clears the front leg and hits me over long-on for a six. It just puts me off my plans, and I start trying to bowl yorkers. He hits the last two balls for sixes, and we are set 24 to win.

I am on my haunches and am scratching my forehead when MS walks past me, making a gesture that I should have bowled the carrom ball. We go on to lose, and I am shattered. MS says nothing; there are no recriminations.

Albie Morkel is big on wildlife and has organized a game ride for the next morning. I tell the team management that I won't be coming along. I am shattered and need some time alone. Albie and Haydos come to my room and tell me, 'You should come. It will be fun. Don't lock yourself away.'

I don't go anyway. Later in the day, I go for a walk along the sea, ruminating and introspecting. The next day, when we get together for training again, MS calmly asks me why I didn't bowl the carrom ball. I tell him I thought about it, but somehow I felt like I have been given the responsibility of bowling a big over and I should keep the runs down instead of going for wickets.

MS says, 'The carrom ball is your best ball. If you bowl that and get hit, I have no problems. You should always bowl your best ball. The rest is not in your hands. I gave the over to you because you are very gutsy and I knew you would execute under pressure, but you let yourself down by not backing your guts and your best delivery. Keep that in mind next time.'

Sure enough, the next game against the Warriors is on the line and MS gives me the 18th over. They have two set batters and need just 32 in the last three overs, two of which have to be bowled my me and Murali.

Second ball of the over, I bowl a slow carrom ball. Justin Kruesch wants to hit a six but plays entirely down the wrong line. With the last ball of the over, I get the dangerous Mark Boucher with the carrom ball. MS has a 'told-you-so' look when he tells me, 'You have got too much ability and guts to back down under pressure. Always keep that in mind.'

We come up against the Warriors again in the final. I take out the highest run-getter of the tournament at that time, Davy Jacobs, with an offbreak, and Johan Botha with the carrom ball in a match analysis of 4-0-16-2. M. Vijay and Michael Hussey are too experienced to give us any scares in a chase of 129. Vijay is the Player of the Match, and I am the Player of the Series for being the highest wicket-taker of the tournament. CSK supremacy. Tamil Nadu supremacy.

12

Timing doesn't seem to be my strongest suit right now. When I performed well in the IPL, the team for the T20 World Cup had already been selected. Now my Champions League Player-of-the-Series performance has come after the Test side for the two home Tests against Australia has been announced.

I get the next best thing: a place in the Rest of the India side for the Irani Cup to be played in Jaipur on the same dates as the first Test. It is a match between the Ranji Champions, which is Mumbai in this case, and a side built of the best available players from the rest of the country. Once again, I am to play under Yuvraj Singh.

By now, Yuvraj has seen me bowl in the IPL and Champions League too. Nonetheless, when I bowl to him in the nets, Yuvi Pa is surprised. He asks me, 'What is this? Why are you bowling like this?'

He is referring to my bowling action, which is completely different from the way I bowl in limited-overs cricket. I began working on this last year as another practical hack. I was doing decently well in limited-overs cricket, but I felt I could do more with the red ball: impart more revolutions and draw more out of the ball in the air.

This action is my version of what Sunny Gupta does at MRF's team, the Globe Trotters, in the TNCA league. He is a beautiful bowler with a lovely action, which gives him nice drift and dip. His loading and cocking of the wrist are different from mine. I try to copy it, and now my load-up is much higher than in my limited-overs action. I try to get the right wrist in that position where my elbow and the hand are probably parallel to the ground; the load-up going higher is just a by-product. This helps me turn my wrist 180 degrees, letting me impart more revolutions on the ball.

I tell Yuvi Pa that this is how I bowl in first-class cricket. I take two wickets in the first innings and five in the second as we beat Mumbai comfortably. I get Ajinkya Rahane in both innings. He has just scored a hundred in the warm-up match against the Australians and has narrowly missed out on Test selection himself. Yuvi Pa, who scores a double century himself, tells me at the end of the match that I am a really good bowler and that he is looking forward to seeing me in India colours.

Which is ironic because I've already played for India, but perhaps it didn't get noticed because it was in Zimbabwe. Yuvi Pa's wish is soon fulfilled with my selection for the ODIs against Australia. The main Test bowlers, including Harbhajan Singh, have been rested so that they can be ready for the upcoming Test series against New Zealand.

This series feels like a second debut, but it almost doesn't happen. Two of the three matches—in Kochi and Goa—are washed out, but the east coast provides us with better weather in Vizag. We win the game with a superb Virat Kohli century. I get Michael Hussey out in figures of 9-0-34-1.

When most of the Test players leave early for South Africa, we still have five ODIs at home against New Zealand. This is my first big, consistent chance. MS is not there, so Gautam Gambhir is the captain. Gautam and I have a great camaraderie, as he understands spin bowling. He knows me well from having faced me in the nets over the past year or so.

In the first match, Gautam gets me into the game pretty early. He knows I like bowling with the hard new ball. He brings me on in the eighth over and asks me what field I want. I tell him I want mid-on up, and square leg and cow corner back. I have always had this fascination with tempting batters to go over mid-on, and then dropping the length and getting them to drag their shot to cow corner. Raman always used to suggest that field. Gauti says to take long-on and deep midwicket. 'Let him sweep. If you feel like he is going to sweep, use your other ball.'

I just look at him, and he says, 'Ash, just bowl the way you want. Just enjoy and bowl. Four and sixes is fine, man. Anyone can hit you, but I know you will get me the wickets.'

In my second over, I get Martin Guptill, who tries to go over mid-off because mid-on is back. We have New Zealand struggling in the chase of 277, but they still have a set Ross Taylor and a potentially dangerous Gareth Hopkins left. In the 34th over, they call for the batting powerplay. This is a period of five overs where you are allowed only three fielders outside the circle as opposed to five. Teams tend to do so between the 30th and 40th overs because they are going to hit out in the last 10 anyway.

As soon as the fielding restrictions are imposed, Gautam turns to me to bowl. Taylor hits me for a six second ball, but I come back to dismiss him with a carrom ball the next ball.

Ashish Nehra is the other bowler entrusted with these tough overs. He draws a chance from Hopkins on a short ball, which if taken seals the game, but I fail to catch it. I sight the ball well, get into a good position, and put my hands up in the right place for the catch, but the ball hits my hands and parries away for a four. Ashish is really angry. He's already had one catch dropped off his bowling.

Luckily, I manage to get Hopkins in the next over, bringing a smile to Ashish's face. I have figures of 10-1-50-3. Gautam makes it a point at the post-match presentation to mention my performance, but all I can think of is the dropped catch. I just can't enjoy the night because of the catch.

I am aware that I carry the reputation of not being a great fielder. This baggage has followed me since my Under-14 days. I am not the quickest on the park, but I've always been a good catcher. I've fielded at slip with distinction and have even put in extra effort to get quicker on the field.

In fact, as far back as my last year of school, on rainy days I would go out and practise sliding on wet grass because I wanted to make up a few yards. However, people have found it hard to distinguish a good and safe fielder from a downright poor fielder just because they aren't quick and agile. A poor fielder is someone who fumbles balls, has a poor throw, and drops catches. I do none of that, but this tag has always been around my neck.

Even in the IPL, M.S. Dhoni put me in slightly safer places. Once MS saw my efforts in the field, he started putting me in slightly better areas. It can all be self-perpetuating. If you encourage people to stand in difficult areas and tell them they're good, they get better. But if you say you're bad by indicating that you only field in safer areas, not only does it become a psychological thing, but other captains also tend to do that.

I have come to the Indian team with that pressure at the back of my mind. When I drop that catch, it only gets worse. 'Oh, I've dropped a catch at the international level. This will further stick to my name, and it will just keep getting bigger.'

From the extremely humid conditions of Guwahati, we go to the bone-dry city of Jaipur, which is even drier in the early winters. I generally struggle in dry conditions because the ball just slips out of my fingers. I need some humidity to get some grip on the ball.

Perennial calluses on the fingers are part of every bowler's life, more so for finger spinners. I am no different. Except that in dry conditions, they turn completely white and numb. I like to grip the ball tight, deep in my long fingers, so that I can spin it hard. In dry conditions, though, I don't even feel the ball in my fingers because of the thick calluses, and the ball just slips out.

I am worried about this when Gauti gets me on in the 14th over. My worst fear comes true because the ball is just not coming out right. It takes me a good two-three overs to find my rhythm. I make a mental note to make sure I keep my hands moisturized beforehand whenever playing in dry places.

Gauti calls me back the moment New Zealand ask for the batting powerplay in the 37th over, and again, I get him a wicket immediately. This time, a set Guptill with the carrom ball.

For now, my fielding is not cause for concern for the rest of the series. We win 5-0, and I end up with more wickets than anyone. In three matches, Gauti calls upon me as soon as New Zealand opt for the batting powerplay. In the other two, their innings doesn't last long enough for them to think of it.

Gauti, who has scored two quality hundreds, is the Player of the Series. After receiving the award and finishing his interviews, he tells me, 'I may have received the Player-of-the-Series award, but it really should have been you. You're the one who actually won us the series. I'm not saying it because you're new or anything like that, but your 10 overs neatly stacked up into various difficult phases throughout the series. You really deserved it. Well done.'

Gauti doesn't have to tell me this, but he does. I feel really special because of the faith the captain has in my bowling. He makes it a point to praise me in public, too. 'If you have an offspinner who can bowl well in the powerplays and slog overs, it can be a great asset for the team,' he says at the press conference.

While the Test matches are on in South Africa, I am now named in a full-strength squad for the limited-overs matches in South Africa. For the first time, I actually begin to consider what Gary told me in South Africa: I could be going to the World Cup.

* * *

In the middle of the South Africa tour, two days before the third ODI in Cape Town, I am sitting by myself at the breakfast table when a large, moustached man approaches me. He says hello in a burly voice. That voice might as well be Military Uncle's.

I reply, 'Hello sir.'

Then, he congratulates me. I ask, 'What happened?'

'You don't know?' the man says. 'You have been selected for the World Cup, young man.'

After the New Zealand series, I always thought I stood a good chance. While this is not a surprise, you only believe it when the name is actually announced. I don't have to wait long for a written confirmation. The next morning, a newspaper is slid under my hotel room door. It is a copy of *The Daily Telegraph* from Kolkata. The team news article mentions how the journalist saw this young man, Ashwin, at the breakfast table and conveyed the good news to him. That the journalist was the first person to inform Ashwin of his selection. It was written by Lokendra Pratap Sahi.

Rohit Sharma misses out on the selection, but the next day he goes out to open for the first time in ODI cricket. That slot, anyway, belongs to three men: Virender Sehwag, Sachin Tendulkar and Gautam Gambhir. We go on to win a tight match, with Yusuf Pathan and Bhajju Pa starring with both bat and ball.

We go to Port Elizabeth with a 2-1 series lead. It is a hot, muggy afternoon at St George's Park. There is no power in whole of Port Elizabeth at the time of the start of the match. So no national anthems are sung, and their signature brass band is in full flow. I am running the drinks.

I take water. MS drinks. Two overs later, I take more. He drinks more. Then again. I have carried more water for MS than anyone else. When I go in for the drink break, MS asks, 'Where is Sree?'

It is possibly the most neutral way of asking a question. It is also the MS way. You just can't make out why he is asking. I don't know what to tell him because I don't know what it might lead to. MS insists on finding out. I tell him Sree is upstairs in the dressing room. He tells me to tell Sree he has to come down and sit with the other reserves.

Sree is Sreesanth, the most gifted fast bowler I have seen in person. He is also a temperamental character. On this tour, he once took me out like I was his best friend. He insisted I go with him and learn how to socialize. We had a great time, and he even hugged me goodbye. The next morning, he looked right through me like he had never met me.

Anyway, on the way back from the drinks break, I am wondering how, while keeping wicket in an international match, MS even noticed that Sree was not sitting downstairs. I go back and tell M. Vijay, who is in his cooling glasses with his feet up on another chair, 'Hey, Monk, MS asked Sree to come down.'

Monk tells me, 'Hey, you go and tell him. Don't expect me to do that.'

I quickly run up because you never know when MS might need another drink. I go into the changing room and find Sree buck naked, getting a massage. I tell him, 'Sree, MS wants you to come down.'

'Why? You can't carry water?'

I tell him I didn't say anything. He said he wants you to come down. He said the reserves should be together for the game.

Sree says, 'Okay, you go. I will come.'

I return to my drink duties. The next time I have to go with a helmet. This time I can sense MS is angry, and I have never seen him lose his cool. 'Where is Sree? What is he doing?' MS asks sternly.

I tell him he is getting a massage. MS doesn't say anything.

In the next over, he calls me to return the helmet. He is calm now. While giving me the helmet, he says, 'Do one thing. Go to Ranjib sir. Tell him Sree is not interested in being here. Ask him to book his ticket for tomorrow so he can go back to India.'

I am stunned. I'm not sure what to say. I am just staring at his face. MS goes, 'What happened? You don't understand English either now?'

Ranjib Biswal is our manager on tour. I am not sure I should go to him. This time I quickly run up again and tell Sree that MS is very angry. That he's saying Sree can take the next flight home. Sree quickly gets up and gets dressed.

Not only that, but now he assumes the drinks duties. The next time MS needs a drink, Sree makes sure he charges out. Instead of taking the drink from him, MS motions for me to come over. 'Did you tell Ranjib sir or not?' he asks me.

I have no option but to tell Ranjib sir. I also give Sree the look that says, 'What else could I do?' I am also reminded of the Duleep Trophy final, when he bowled legbreaks with the first new ball. Or the time when I captained him in a Deodhar Trophy match, the one-day version of the Duleep Trophy. Abhinav Mukund and myself rescued us from 79 for 5 to post 222 on a difficult wicket, but Sree bowled four leg breaks in the first three overs. He went for 52 in his seven overs.

MS and Sree sort it out later, but during that period I am caught in a situation in which I would ideally be laughing but am too scared to do so.

In the next match, in Centurion, Hashim Amla scores an unbeaten hundred. At some point in the innings, we need a substitute fielder. Seeing that Monk has gone up for a toilet break, I run out. Rohit is bowling his part-time offspin, and MS places me at short square leg. The fourth ball is a long hop, and Hashim wallops a pull. I have no time to react. I dive and get to it, but the ball hits my hand and wobbles out. Six balls I go out for, I get a catch, and I drop it. I haven't yet taken a catch in international cricket. I am the same guy who celebrated hard when I took MS's catch in the Challenger Trophy.

At the end of the game, I tell Gary I am distraught. I tell him I will work harder on my fielding and that they shouldn't feel the need to hide me when they pick me. What I probably mean is that I don't want to miss out on being selected because of perceptions about my fielding.

* * *

When I return home, Vicky tells me about Military Uncle. He says he texts him every time I do well. Once, he got so excited, he started calling just after I had bowled a maiden over. 'What does he think you leave your phone with the umpire with your cap or what?' I ask Vicky to keep returning the texts with thanks and tell him it is difficult to take the calls. He has only been a well-wisher, even if a little intrusive.

As the World Cup draws nearer, the frenzy in India is going wild. So much so that Raju the dreamer of the RUCA team, calls me on Skype in South Africa and tells me about a TV ad campaign called 'Change the Game'. It is based on signature innovative shots or balls. Viru Pa is there with his upper cut, Kevin Pietersen has the switch hit, Tillakaratne Dilshan is featured with his ramp called the 'Dilscoop', Bhajju Pa has his *doosra* and MS has the helicopter shot.

Raju is in a frenzy himself because he believes he has something that should be featured in the campaign. He calls it the 'slingshot ball', and says he slings it like Malinga but bowls it like an undercutter. I ask him what the ball does. He says that is why he has called me on Skype—to show it to me. The ball pitches and skids away from the right-hand bat. It's almost an underarm delivery that works on a 12-yard concrete strip inside the house.

Raju goes on to tell me that he is feeling generous and will let me use that ball to pitch it to Pepsi, who are running the campaign. I wonder how I will repay this debt. I ask him what else is happening in his life, and he tells me about the movie scripts he's written. He's even worked out the budgets down to which parts of the movie will cost how many lakhs. He's decided which actors he is going to cast as the hero and the heroine. More people that will be indebted to Raju.

13

There is a certain comfort in going back to the National Cricket Academy in Bangalore. Ever since it replaced the makeshift dormitories under the stands at M. Chinnaswamy Stadium, the NCA has not changed one bit. It is like a second home for so many cricketers.

We are here for a five-day camp, which will lead to a warm-up match against Australia before we travel to Dhaka for the start of the World Cup. It is a rigorous camp. MS has asked me to keep working on the carrom ball but not to bowl it too much in the nets. He probably doesn't want the mystery to wear off because he has to use me against these same batters in the IPL. He also tells me to work on lines that always keep the stumps in play.

Apart from bowling a lot on these five days, I spend extra time working on the other two aspects of the game that give me anxiety. Your fielding and batting can sometimes be the tiebreaker when it comes to selection, so I don't want to leave any stone unturned there.

I've entered international cricket thinking I am a good batter against pace, and while I can be an uncertain starter against them, I rate myself pretty highly against spinners once I am in. So far, I have batted only twice in international cricket, so I haven't had the opportunity to test myself out there. MS probably thinks I am a proper tailender and not someone who started out as a batter.

Our team doesn't carry the sidearm, the dog-thrower, that some teams have started using to simulate high pace in the nets. Our way of doing it is with the bowling machine, but the batters prefer to face Gary Kirsten, who runs in four paces and chucks the ball furiously at them from 16 yards. His forty-three-year-old shoulder gets a thorough workout because batters at the top level are insatiable.

I may have been around for a year and a half, but I have faced Gary only once because those throwdowns are a precious commodity reserved for the playing XI, and even among them the specialist batters. It was in Dambulla, and I found him to be really quick.

At this camp, I get to face Gary's throwdowns properly for the first time. I struggle for time when facing him. I have never felt short on time in first-class cricket. Ashok Dinda and Munaf Patel are the quickest I have faced in first-class cricket and have never struggled for pace. If they bounce, I deliberately hook them in the air so that the top edge can clear the field.

Facing Gary, I realize I can't afford to stay still and play like I do in first-class cricket. Against high pace, you need an early preparatory movement so you are not hurried. When they say you get used to pace once you face it, what really happens is you start making the correct preparatory movement and start timing it perfectly. Some do it even without realizing they are doing it; I do it consciously.

I ask the team analyst, C.K.M. Dhananjai, to film me when I am facing Gary. When I watch it, I realize how late I am, and I need that initial preparatory movement just at the time of release. The idea is to have made half of your movements already, so you have more time to face the ball. Even the most gifted batters, who might pick the ball sooner than anyone else, need that trigger movement against extreme pace. I can feel the improvement when facing Gary at the end of this camp.

We are not big on warm-ups with other sports before getting into the day's work. On the odd occasion, we may play some football, but warming up is largely an individual activity. I use that period when my attendance is not mandatory to run off to R. Sridhar at NCA to work on the other aspect that makes me anxious.

Sridhar, a former Hyderabad player, is now a coach at NCA. He speaks Tamil. I find it easier to open myself up to him. I pour my heart out, telling him how bad I feel that I have not taken a single catch in international cricket in one and a half years. He asks me not to fuss unnecessarily. He tells me it is just two catches that have come my way. He says he has seen me field, I am a good catcher, I have big hands, and all these things are psychological. We will do repetitions every day, and we will mix the drill. I go into the World Cup with my confidence somewhat restored.

Our first match is a bit of a banana peel. Playing the World Cup opener against Bangladesh in front of a raucous home crowd is no easy task. They beat us in the last World Cup. They have just beaten New Zealand 4-0 at home.

Viru Pa makes an emphatic statement first ball after Bangladesh ask us to bat first. It is a good ball, but he smashes it off the back foot through covers for four. The silence is deafening. In the lead-up to the World Cup, he said in the press that he wanted to bat all 50 overs. He gets out in the 48th over, having scored 175. Virat Kohli also gets a hundred, and we set them 371. Bangladesh make us work hard for the win. They are not a side to be taken lightly at this World Cup.

This team under MS is not big on meetings. His contribution to all meetings is, 'All good, let's go.' Gary doesn't do big meetings either. We're all surprised when Gary calls everyone for a meeting the day after we get to Bangalore. Our next match, against England, is still a week away. This can, for all intents and purposes, be called an emergency meeting.

When we get to the team room in the hotel, Gary says Viru Pa will lead this meeting. He is sitting right next to me, and then he gets up and starts talking in a serious tone. Being a straight shooter, he cuts straight to the chase. He says we are not being given our usual quota of five match tickets that we can give away to our friends and family. We're getting only three tickets each, which is unacceptable.

Ranjib Biswal, the manager, tries to explain to him that because this is a World Cup, the demand for tickets is huge, and we've been given only three each.

Viru Pa casually says, 'It is we who are playing. If we don't play, there will be no demand for these tickets.'

Gary tries to calm him down by saying that he and the entire support staff don't have any family travelling, so they are happy to give up their tickets. Viru Pa refuses, saying he wants what he is owed. 'You will give me extra tickets because I am a senior,' he says. 'But what about Ash? He is a new boy. He should also get his full share. No, Ash?'

Viru Pa then looks at me. Am I expected to respond? I don't know what to say and don't want to be caught in any cross hairs, but I, of course, nod in agreement. Ranjib sir is forced to immediately make calls, and he assures us that everyone will get the usual quota of five tickets each.

MS doesn't need to end this meeting with an 'All good, let's go'.

* * *

We are in Bangalore for over two weeks for just two games. Our next match is a week away. I am quite bored staying at the hotel. This stay is unlike any I've had in Bangalore when I could go out. This time, it feels like we are caged in our hotels.

I haven't even met Prithi in a long time. We've just been talking on the phone. Now that there is free time, I start thinking about my relationship with her. I haven't been friend-zoned yet, but I'm not quite her boyfriend either. It is a very disturbing situation for me. She hasn't told me off, so I have hope, but why is she not comfortable taking our relationship forward? Am I doing the right thing? Am I wasting my time? Do I even make her feel as special as she makes me feel?

Eventually, I pick up the phone and call her. During our conversations, I've had a feeling she would like me to be introduced to her dad too. It is just a hunch, but I act on it. I call her father too, greet him, and tell him that Prithi and I are friends and that we've known each other since our school days. When I speak to Prithi next, I ask her if she would like to come to the matches so we can hang out. I tell her about how Viru Pa has made sure I get all five of my complimentary tickets.

Prithi agrees to come and join me at some point during the World Cup.

* * *

Sreesanth went for 53 in five overs in Bangladesh. Against England, he has been left out for a spinner, but that spinner is not me. It is Piyush Chawla.

Again, Viru Pa starts with a four, but this time thanks to a drop by Graeme Swann at second slip. Today Paaji scores a hundred as we give England a stiff 339. It doesn't look stiff in the evening, though. Andrew Strauss and Kevin Pietersen get off to a quick start. Strauss goes on to bat long, and is cruising to the target in a big partnership with Ian Bell.

I sit next to Sree, who keeps telling me, 'Gone Machan.' When I run the drinks, though, I hear MS telling the team that this match will turn. He firmly believes it, and he just keeps telling the guys that there is a Zak spell to come. That the ball will reverse swing here. He actually tells them not to go looking for a wicket but to leave Zak something to work with if the ball does reverse.

Sure enough, it reverses, and Zak gets Strauss with a reverse-swinging yorker. I tell Sree what MS has been saying, and we cheer on. Then Zak gets Paul Collingwood with a knuckle-ball slower ball, which he has been working on in the nets. Munaf Patel follows up the good work with a quiet over, but we still have one over of spin left. England target Piyush in that over. They hit Piyush for two sixes, but he gets Tim Bresnan out with the last ball to keep us in the game. Munaf manages to tie the match in the last over, conceding just 18 in the 48th and 50th overs put together.

The good thing about being in Bangalore, though, is that I keep working on my fielding with Sridhar, apart from batting against Gary's rapid throwdowns.

When we finally play the second game in Bangalore, we are 100 for 4 when chasing 208 against Ireland. Yuvi Pa and MS, though, put together a sedate stand to see us through.

When we go to Delhi to face Netherlands, three of my tickets go to Viru Pa and two to Gauti, both of whom are from Delhi. We still stick with three spinners, including Yuvi Pa, but Ashish Nehra is brought into the picture. MS says at the toss that Piyush needs to get more practice, and that Ashwin is mentally stronger and can fit in at any time, against any opposition.

It pretty much sums up my bowler–captain relationship with MS. I've bowled all the difficult overs for him in the IPL and the Champions League. He knows that Gauti also used me in the batting powerplays against New Zealand when he left early for South Africa. I have seen him hand-hold bowlers, but he's never had to tell me how to bowl or which field to take. He knows if someone can bowl spin regularly with just two boundary riders, he can handle any pressure.

MS knows me inside-out as a person. He often tells me I should not overthink things off the field. On the field, he doesn't tell me how to bowl. It is only me who wants to try many things, and wants to check with MS to make sure I am not overdoing it. His response is always: 'If you want to bowl legspin also, do that. No problem. You are one of the very few guys who can do that. Why clip that creativity?'

The only thing is that, because I bowl most of my overs with no cushion of boundary riders, I have to restrict my creativity. I have to give up some of my variations. My topspinner, for example, has been a good friend, but you just can't bowl it in the powerplay because if it is even a little slow, it can be hit away through the covers off the back foot. You can take that risk in the middle overs because then it just goes for the single.

It feels great that MS is confident enough to just let me be on the field, not because I want to be there but because he recognizes that I can *be*. This public statement of confidence in me at the toss in Delhi makes it even better, but it's not easy to not be playing in a home World Cup.

We lose the toss on a pitch that assists spin and are 99 for 4 chasing 190. Once again, Yuvi Pa takes us home with the bat to go with his two wickets earlier. His bowling had helped keep the target down; otherwise, the chase could have been really tricky.

We go to Nagpur for the game against South Africa, and Appa comes to watch us there. Now MS leaves out Piyush, but not for me. For the first time since Sreesanth in Bangladesh, we are playing with three quicks. It is Munaf who returns this time.

We get a great start, and Paaji goes on to score a century, but we score only 38 runs in the last 11 overs, losing nine wickets. We run South Africa close in defence of 296 and have them down at one point, but Robin Peterson's shots come off against Ashish in the last over.

So now we have tied against England, haven't won comprehensively against Ireland and the Netherlands, and have also lost to South Africa. However, there is no concern within the team. It is all calm and business as usual. Gary just says there is a quality cricket team sitting right here, and he wants to see it in the remaining games.

Gary is always cool and always has a smile on his face. I wonder if he puts that smile on to make sure he is calm and transfers only calmness to the rest of the team. There has been this calmness and belief throughout the whole campaign. Since well before the tournament, Gary and Paddy have been talking about visualising the big matches in front of home crowds. It's almost like no one considers the possibility of not winning. It feels like we are destined to win the World Cup. This loss is not even discussed in the dressing room.

The reaction from South Africa, though, is different. Prasanna Agoram, their analyst from Chennai, is trying to rub it in my face. He is another one of those talented people who don't get appreciated at home. Perhaps he is a bit in your face, which cricketers don't like sometimes, but he is a good analyst. Now he is telling me I should have played. 'Why aren't you playing?' he asks. I don't give him the satisfaction of thinking I'm disappointed. He says this match was big for them. Beating the hosts is a big thing, and now they are going to win the whole thing.

I can see where he is coming from. As an Indian living in South Africa, this is probably a huge game for him because it is against India. Perhaps he wishes to prove a point against a system that doesn't utilize his services. Perhaps they also need a win after losing a tight match to England last week.

When we get to Chennai for our last league game, we've already qualified for the quarter-finals. In fact, qualifying for the next round is not difficult because four out of six teams are going through. However, this match will decide whom we face in the quarter-finals. If we win, we get Australia. If we lose, we get Sri Lanka, but that means we could be facing Australia later. The feeling within the team is that the sooner we get Australia out of the way, the better, because Australia in a big final is something else.

The Chennai track has been helping the spinners all through the World Cup, but this pitch is going to turn much less. Nevertheless, this is my first match of the World Cup. Finally.

MS wins the toss, Yuvi Pa's century takes us to 268, and I am opening the bowling. I take the first and last wickets to fall: opener Kirk Edwards and No. 11 Ravi Rampaul with carrom balls.

Between those two events, Zak bowls a knuckle ball to Ramnaresh Sarwan, and I run to my right from sweeper-cover and take a nice catch. Nobody knows on or off the field, but I am extremely relieved that I have taken my first catch for India. Sarwan c Ashwin b Zaheer is a significant scorecard entry. I have got off my back a monkey that no one even knew existed. Well, apart from Gary and Sridhar.

At the end of the match, Eric Simmons, the bowling coach, tells me, 'Youngster, you were amazing. And this is exactly how we planned it. You will play a very crucial role in winning us the World Cup.'

It sits nicely with my belief that MS and Gary have earmarked me as their surprise weapon in the big matches of the World Cup, and this is why they've been hiding me from the opposition. Behind the scenes, Gary and Paddy have been preparing me since the tri-series in Dambulla last year. Now that the knockouts are here, I am going to be a key player.

And we have our wish. Australia in a quarter-final, and not, say, a final. This is the match they've been preparing me for all this time. After we lose the toss and Australia choose to bat on a pitch that will slow down, I bowl the first over. I take out Shane Watson during the first powerplay and then come back during the batting powerplay to dismiss Ricky Ponting, who has already scored a century. Yuvi Pa gets two big wickets again, those of Michael Clarke and Brad Haddin.

We get a good start in the chase for 261. Looking at the scoreboard, it appears we are in control, but in the dressing room, this is a tense chase, if only because this is Australia. As expected, the game does turn. Gauti and Yuvi are both batting beautifully, but they are not running well.

Gauti gets run out. MS goes out to bat, and I get padded up because Sachin Paaji has told MS I should bat ahead of Harbhajan. Suresh Raina and I are padded up and sitting outside when Paaji comes out to talk. He has a word with Suresh first and then tells me, 'Do you remember that knock against Australia at Bangalore? I believe that against this attack, you've got the batting and the tools. You get this game done for us. You'll be going ahead of Bhajji.'

In the warm-up match, I came in at No. 10, behind both Bhajju Pa and Piyush, but took us from 138 for 8 to 214. It was pretty much the same attack. I find it amazing that Paaji remembers it in such detail.

When MS falls in the 38th over and Suresh goes out to bat, we still need 74 with five wickets in hand. I start getting mentally ready to bat, but Yuvi Pa and Suresh make sure that need doesn't arise. We've knocked out the team that has won the last three World Cups. This is only their second defeat in their last 36 World Cup matches. They may be going through a transition, but they have players who have the experience of being part of that streak. It's just that we have enough quality and experience on our side to beat them.

Yuvi Pa has been the Player of the Match in four of our last five matches. He has done this despite often being unwell. He has been vomiting and has had bouts of coughing. On one occasion, he coughed up blood in the washbasin. After this win, he tells the press he is playing this World Cup for a special person. I don't have the courage to ask him who that special person is or why he has been coughing blood. I have too much respect for these players to cross any lines.

Now that Australia are out of the way, we really begin to consider the enormity of winning the World Cup. The anxiety starts to kick in. We are just two games away. The first one is against Pakistan in Mohali. We have four days in Mohali before the semi-final.

* * *

I ask Prithi to join me for the semi-final match, and she says yes. So I tell Ranjib sir that we need to make arrangements for my girlfriend. He says, 'Girlfriend, huh?' I say yes. He then asks me if I will marry her. I feel the conversation is getting a little weird, but I say yes, or at least I wish to. He asks Prithi the same question after she arrives and I've introduced them. I feel like I am bringing her home to my parents, not my cricket team.

There is excitement as well as anxiety as we train. I'm told I will be playing. We speak about the fields that I will take as I will be bowling in the powerplays. On the morning of the match, Prithi and I meet for breakfast. Prithi asks me if I am feeling the pressure of such a big match. Even before I can answer, I receive a message from Gary. He tells me there was a lot of dew at the ground last night, so they have decided to go with an extra fast bowler. He says I played an incredible role in getting us here.

Then I tell Prithi that I'm not feeling any pressure because I am not playing and that we can chill now. However, that doesn't remain the case for long, as the next message is to assemble early in the team activity room because C.K.M. Dhananjai, our analyst, better known as DJ, is going to show us one of his movies.

DJ has many jobs as an analyst. He films us in the nets. He edits opposition videos for us to study. Gary uses him a lot to identify any technical flaws that could be creeping into any of our games. His biggest job, though, at least according to some of the players, is making these movies.

I get there about half an hour early because, ever since my Tamil Nadu days, I like annoying the analysts. They've been my best buddies because they are also cricket nerds like me. As I can't do all of this in front of the senior players, I make sure to get there early. I find DJ extremely nervous as he sets up the speakers and the projector. The thing with analysts in India is that whenever they make a presentation, more than the content of the presentation, it is important that the presentation works. If it doesn't, they think it is a bad omen.

Even the best cricketers deal with more failures than successes in their careers. We're always looking for answers to why we failed. Sometimes you find the perfect reason, sometimes you can tell yourself the truth, but sometimes the reason is not obvious. You can do everything right and still fail. That's why quite a few cricketers become superstitious and start looking for 'signs' even in retrospect. If this movie doesn't work and we lose, at the end of the day, people can say the day began on an inauspicious note.

These DJ movies are the last thing that should be taken so seriously, but such is the nature of pressure and team sports. These movies are called 'WWW Productions', short for We Will Win. They are mostly musicals. There is a story arc and a lot of music, but the actors are us, either recorded in the nets or from match footage.

WWW Productions deals in all genres including slapstick comedies, where editing tools are used to make us look weirdly shaped, like in distorting mirrors. The team, full of mature, competitive people who do what a very select bunch of people in the world can do, laughs at these like kids watching cartoons. Then there are emotional redemptive tales with music that tugs at the heartstrings, where he picks out shots of when we were at a low and ends it with celebration. There are documentaries where he intends to make us think about something.

DJ takes the help of his backend team for editing, but all the concepts are his. That is a time-consuming affair, which is why he saves them for big occasions. Sometimes a player might pull his leg and tell him, 'Hey DJ, we hardly see you work these days. When is the next movie?' This, though, is not one of those occasions.

There is a Tamil comedy film from the 1960s called *Kadhalikka Neramillai* that has endured over the decades. The comedy character in the movie, played by actor Nagesh, is an aspiring filmmaker whose production house doesn't have any finances and is called 'Oho Productions'. I ask DJ, 'What is the plan for Oho Productions today?'

Oho Productions sounds more like something Raju should run and not the excellent analyst of a high-performing cricket team. I genuinely don't rate the impact these presentations have. However, I have seen in the past the positive effect it has on the players. Some leave them with actual goosebumps. Players love to watch themselves on screen. Here are people who are super high-performance athletes, but they want it spelt out on the screen. They want to be the centre of attention. They want to be heroes. They want to feel like movie stars.

DJ tells me Oho Productions has done a full commercial entertainer for today. It again tells me it is a big occasion, and DJ is playing it safe. Commercial entertainers rarely go wrong. This one has footage from our wins and from the nets. It has all the big hits: sixes, fours, wickets and celebrations. In the background plays the song *Chak De India*, which used to play in the stands during the 2007 T20 World Cup, which we won. It ends with a photo of Yuvi Pa celebrating the win against Australia.

Everyone is pumped up after watching it. DJ is relieved that nothing went wrong during the presentation. After the show is over, Gary says the support staff is mostly non-Indian. They value this team, and it's a big game for them too, but they can't even begin to imagine how big playing Pakistan in a World Cup is for us players. He says they're all leaving now, so we can be alone and conduct the rest of the meeting ourselves.

I'm a huge cynic of these presentations and meetings where actual cricket is not discussed, but even I begin to see the impact of this meeting two hours before the match. Paaji speaks first. He goes into the past, talks about what the journey has been like and how during every single game and moment in the last two to three years, he has thought about playing a semi-final or a final against Pakistan in the 2011 World Cup and beating them to lift the trophy. Everyone speaks. It is raw and emotional. The connect has happened.

Finally, it is MS's turn to speak. He says, 'All good, let's go.'

Prithi is joined by Appa and two of my friends in the stands. They haven't had to buy tickets because they're from my complimentary allotment. I doubt their preparation for the match is this dramatic. It is deafening when we get to the ground. The Who's Who of politics, society and Bollywood is attending. We are introduced to the prime ministers of both countries minutes before the start, just in case we didn't feel the enormity of the occasion.

We win the toss and bat first. Once again, like in the match against South Africa, we are losing wickets in a rush after the good start provided by Paaji and Viru Pa. We get only 260 after looking good for 300 at one point.

Misbah-ul-Haq is a little like MS. He, too, likes to take games deep. He nearly beat us single-handedly in the 2007 T20 World Cup final. He makes a slow start, just looking to absorb the pressure, but we keep chipping away at the wickets. Then, with 93 required in the last 11, he reverse sweeps Yuvi Pa for a four out of the blue. There's also a batting powerplay to come when we will have only three fielders outside the circle. Misbah is playing it smartly, but we are getting his partners out.

Ashish, my replacement for the match because of the dew, injures himself badly trying to take a low catch from Shahid Afridi. He has been bowling beautifully, though. His first seven overs have gone for just 24. MS has put his trust in Ashish for the final few overs. Zaheer and Ashish close the game for us, taking us to the final in Mumbai.

Before that, though, we need to make it to the hotel in Chandigarh, a short drive away on a normal day, but this is no normal day. There is a sea of people accompanying our team bus. Prithi and my friends don't find any transport, so they decide to walk. Our bus is not going much faster than walking. And people are walking with us.

There is a whole new crowd waiting just to catch a glimpse of us at almost 2 a.m., when we finally make it to the hotel. Prithi makes it an hour later because there is no room to walk either.

* * *

At our first training session at Wankhede, MS speaks to me. He explains the selection in Mohali, and says Ashish is ruled out because of his broken finger. He tells me I could be playing the final, and asks me not to be overawed by the occasion. He also tells me it's just another game and that, with my skills, I should be fine.

Appa attended the England, South Africa and Pakistan matches, apart from attending the West Indies match in Chennai. He is not here for the final, though. Prithi makes it. I am all pumped up. At the last minute, though, they make the decision to play Sreesanth, just in case we lose the toss and have to bowl in possible dew.

Zak has a great start, Yuvi Pa takes two wickets again, and we are set 275. Lasith Malinga bowls just as well as Zak did, and we lose Viru Pa and Paaji early. Gauti and Virat revive the innings, MS promotes himself ahead of Yuvi Pa. The dew becomes a clear and significant factor in the second half of the chase. He looks at complete ease against Murali, his CSK teammate. Gauti misses out on a hundred, but his wicket means the biggest hero of the tournament, Yuvi Pa, is in the middle when MS hits Nuwan Kulasekara for the final six.

I can't begin to imagine what a huge moment this is for those players who couldn't even get to their homes for days after the early exit in the 2007 World Cup. There is so much joy that everyone is in tears. I can understand the emotion of those who were there in 2007, but it is so moving that Virat, Suresh and even our masseur, Amit Shah, are weeping. Only Ramji Srinivasan, our trainer, and I are not that emotional. We observe all this with mild amusement and a lot of awe.

Soon, a champagne bottle is opened, we take photos with the trophy, and before we know it, it is 2 a.m. Amid all this, Gary finds the time to sit me down for a chat.

'Boy, I'm telling you, you're a really, really special cricketer,' Gary tells me. 'The kind of strides you made from 2009 to 2011 in every aspect of your game . . . See, everyone comes in here with what they're good at and also their weaknesses. They continue to play to their strengths, and they try to hide their weaknesses, but very few come in with their strengths, evolve with their strengths, know what their weaknesses are, and work on those weaknesses.'

'And I haven't seen another cricketer who has come into the team as a youngster and, within the first two years, spotted their weaknesses and kept ironing them out. You've got a great career ahead of you. You must retain this attribute.'

It's a goosebumps moment for me. It is all sinking in. Now the nameplate can say, 'R. Ashwin. World Cup champion.'

* * *

We leave Wankhede at 2.30 a.m., and still, the bus can't move through the streets. People are lined along the whole route towards the team's hotel. There are all kinds of cars stranded: Mercedeses, BMWs, Audis and several others of Indian make. People are dancing on top of these cars, and nobody seems to mind. I gaze outside in wonder. I can't imagine such a moment ever before or again.

It takes an hour and a half to complete the two-kilometre journey to the hotel. At the hotel, the party moves to Paaji's room. I spend a bit of time there and crash in my room.

The next day we are taken to the president's place for felicitation. MS turns up with his head shaved. The next morning, a Tuesday, Prithi and I go back to Chennai because on Thursday I have to report at Chepauk as CSK begin the IPL title defence on Saturday.

Before all that, though, I have to get home. Prithi and I land and take a taxi big enough to accommodate my kitbag and suitcase. I plan to drop Prithi on the way, but she says I should get down first.

We can't get past the Postal Colony 1st Street in West Mambalam, which is a good 300 metres from home. The street is jampacked with people. A couple of people turn up and take the kitbag and suitcase, hold it overhead and pass it along from one person to another. 'Don't worry, anna, it will reach your home safely,' I hear.

It is absolute mayhem. I walk through the crowd, everybody wants to shake my hand, in between I am carried overhead like those pop stars who jump into the crowd at concerts. It takes me half an hour to get home where ten to fifteen news cameras are waiting.

Apart from the media people, random people from the neighbourhood are sitting on the sofa. Amma gives me a stare to tell me to not be rude to anyone. I show Thatha the winning medal. Then Appa and Amma take a look at it. Eventually the bags make their way an hour later.

By the time I have greeted all the neighbours and the media, it has been three hours. When I finally get a moment to myself, I look out at the still-crowded 1st Street of Ramakrishnapuram. I think of all the cricket we have played there, of all the time spent with my friends, of the young man who told me I should have just dropped and run.

Scan QR code to access the
Penguin Random House India website